# THE BIG BOOK OF
# PREHISTORIC LIFE

## DOUGAL DIXON

GALLERY BOOKS
An Imprint of W. H. Smith Publishers Inc.
112 Madison Avenue
New York City 10016

First published in the United States in 1990 by Gallery Books,
an imprint of W.H. Smith Publishers, Inc.,
112 Madison Avenue, New York, New York 10016

By arrangement with The Octopus Publishing Group Limited,
Michelin House, 81 Fulham Road, London SW3 6RB

ISBN 0-8317-0862-X

Printed in Great Britain by BPCC Paulton Books Ltd

Gallery Books are available for bulk purchase for sales promotions and
premium use. For details write or telephone the Manager of Special
Sales, W.H. Smith Publishers, Inc., 112 Madison Avenue, New York,
New York 10016. (212) 532-6600

# CONTENTS

# LIFE'S ORIGIN

T he Earth came into existence
about 4,500 million years ago. It
started off as a disc-shaped cloud of
dust and gas spinning in space. This
cloud then began to gather into lumps,
with a big lump forming in the
middle. The masses of dust began to
heat up and melt with the force of the
particles falling together. Eventually
the big mass at the center became the
Sun. The smaller masses became the
Earth and the other planets spinning
around the Sun.

Life seems to have developed on
the Earth as soon as it was cool
enough. By 3,500 million years ago,
steam from volcanoes had produced
vapor in the early atmosphere, and
some of this had condensed to form
the first oceans in the hot hollows of
the surface. The first living things,
merely complex chemical molecules

that could reproduce themselves, survived there. Simple chemicals were dissolved from the hot rocks by the cooling water, or brought down to the Earth by falling comets and meteorites. The molecules of these chemicals would have been linked together – perhaps by the energy of lightning flashes, perhaps by the ultra-violet rays of the fierce Sun – to produce complicated molecules like those that make up living things today. A basic living molecule like this would have resembled a virus.

These living things only survived if they reproduced themselves accurately, or produced offspring that were better at reproducing than they were. The whole evolution of life on Earth had begun.

**Left:** The early Earth was a bleak and violent place. The surface rocks were still cooling when the first oceans formed, and the atmosphere was full of steam and poisonous gases. Volcanoes rumbled and blasted, and lightning storms raged. Yet, in this turbulent environment, chemical reactions took place that led to the production of the first living things, and so life evolved.

# FOSSILS – EARTH'S CEMETERY

S ome of the animals and plants that lived in the past have left their remains in the rocks, and we can see these remains even after hundreds of millions of years. Sometimes, but not very often, a whole animal is preserved. We sometimes find mammoths – big hairy elephants that lived in the Ice Age – preserved in frozen mud, after falling into bogs about 20,000 years ago.

More often it is only the hard part of the creature that is left. Muds that were formed on the sea bed in the last 50 million years are often full of sharks' teeth. The bodies of the sharks have rotted away.

Often only some of the original substance is left. We can sometimes see the black outline of a leaf in a rock. This is the original carbon of the leaf, all the other leafy substances having decayed away. Coal forms in this way.

Sometimes, when mud containing a piece of wood turns to rock, the minerals in the rock seep into the wood and change it. In the resulting petrified wood, we can see the wood's microscopic structure, but it is now made of mineral.

If the fossil rots away after the mud turns to rock, it leaves a hole called a mold. Water passing through can fill the mold with minerals. The result is a mineral lump in the exact same shape, called a cast. Unlike something petrified, a cast does not show the original internal structure.

Animals' footprints or worm burrows that have turned to stone are called trace fossils.

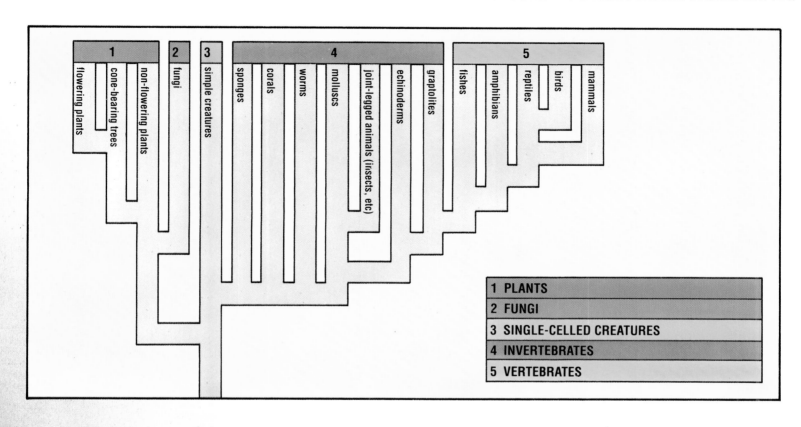

| | | |
|---|---|---|
| **1** | PLANTS | |
| **2** | FUNGI | |
| **3** | SINGLE-CELLED CREATURES | |
| **4** | INVERTEBRATES | |
| **5** | VERTEBRATES | |

**Above:** After two centuries of research, scientists have developed a family tree of living things. They have examined the fossils of extinct creatures, studied how they resemble or differ from the creatures that exist today, and have worked out how they are related. For example, we, as mammals, can trace our ancestry back through reptiles, amphibians, and fish, and even back to the branch of the tree that gave rise to the echinoderms or starfish.

**Left:** A fossil is a beautiful thing in itself, whether it is the delicate impression of a microscopic shell or the bones of a vast dinosaur. A mounted skeleton in a museum is a most impressive sight, and it helps us to understand how life developed on this Earth, over the last millions of years.

# GEOLOGICAL TIME

When we talk about the age of the Earth and of all the different things that lived at different times, we are talking about hundreds of millions of years. To make this easier, scientists divide up the Earth's history into different periods and give these periods a specific scientific name. The periods are based on the different kinds of animals that lived at the time.

By far the biggest section of geological time, about seven-eighths of it, is called the Pre-Cambrian. All things that date from before 590 million years ago – the rocks that formed at that time, and the animals that lived in the seas then – are Pre-Cambrian. We do not find many fossils in the rocks dating from this ancient period because it was so long ago that none of the creatures had evolved shells by that time. They all had soft bodies that usually rotted away before they could be fossilized.

At the beginning of the Cambrian period, about 590 million years ago, all kinds of animals developed hard skeletons and shells. From then on, the rocks are full of fossils.

The rocks formed at different times are not found the world over. In one place we find only rocks and fossils of the Permian and Triassic periods. Another place has Triassic and Jurassic rocks. At a third location, we find Jurassic, Cretaceous, and Tertiary rocks. From the individual outcrops like these, scientists have, over the last 150 years, pieced together the history of the Earth and its life.

**Left**: Most fossils are of water-living creatures, such as this 40 million-year-old fish found in the state of Wyoming.

**Left**: Fossils of insects preserved in the semi-precious mineral, amber, are so delicate that they are used in the most lovely jewelry.

**Above**: Fossils of complete skeletons, like this lizard-like creature, are very rare.

**Right**: Eras and periods are the most important divisions in the geological time scale.

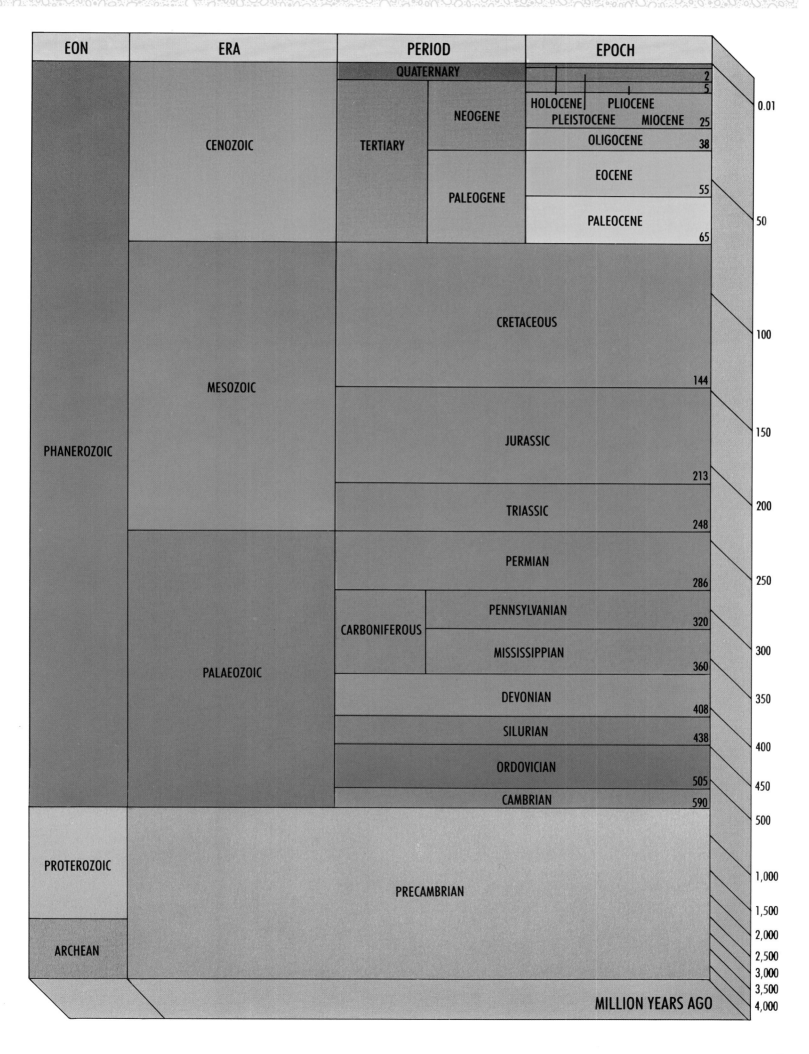

| EON | ERA | PERIOD | EPOCH | |
|---|---|---|---|---|
| PHANEROZOIC | CENOZOIC | QUATERNARY | | 2 |
| | | TERTIARY — NEOGENE | HOLOCENE / PLIOCENE — PLEISTOCENE / MIOCENE | 5 — 25 |
| | | | OLIGOCENE | 38 |
| | | TERTIARY — PALEOGENE | EOCENE | 55 |
| | | | PALEOCENE | 65 |
| | MESOZOIC | CRETACEOUS | | 144 |
| | | JURASSIC | | 213 |
| | | TRIASSIC | | 248 |
| | PALAEOZOIC | PERMIAN | | 286 |
| | | CARBONIFEROUS — PENNSYLVANIAN | | 320 |
| | | CARBONIFEROUS — MISSISSIPPIAN | | 360 |
| | | DEVONIAN | | 408 |
| | | SILURIAN | | 438 |
| | | ORDOVICIAN | | 505 |
| | | CAMBRIAN | | 590 |
| PROTEROZOIC | PRECAMBRIAN | | | |
| ARCHEAN | | | | |

0.01
50
100
150
200
250
300
350
400
450
500
1,000
1,500
2,000
2,500
3,000
3,500
4,000

MILLION YEARS AGO

# PRE-CAMBRIAN STORYBOOK

The oldest rocks on Earth are those that date from Pre-Cambrian times. That is the vast stretch of time reaching from the origin of the Earth right up to about 590 million years ago. The oldest rocks known are in Canada and date from 3,960 million years ago.

Continents consist of flat areas of hard old rocks in the center, surrounded by mountain ranges of younger rocks, with the youngest rocks of all around the outside. The hard old rocks in the hearts of the continents are Pre-Cambrian. They have become compressed and compacted through long years of mountain-building and erosion and are now fused solid. These Pre-Cambrian continental masses are called shields. The old Canadian rocks lie in the Canadian Shield at

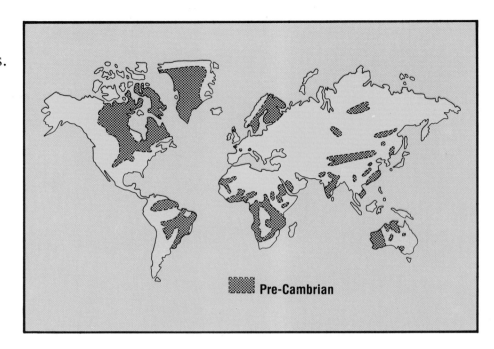

Pre-Cambrian

**Above:** All the continents have Pre-Cambrian cores. The younger rocks accumulated gradually around the edges.

**Below:** Most rocks of the Pre-Cambrian period now form crumpled, eroded landscapes in the hearts of continents, as here in Canada.

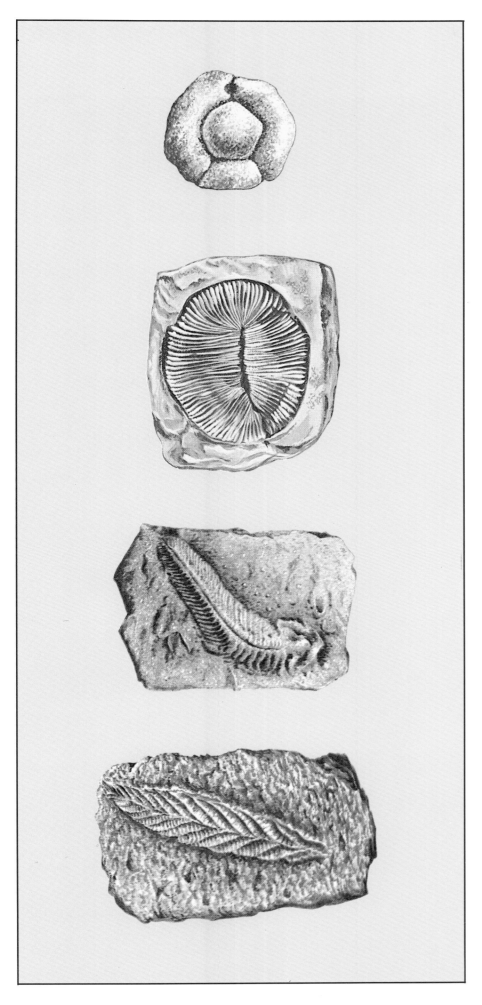

the heart of the North American continent around Hudson Bay.

Most Pre-Cambrian rocks have had a very long history. Many are so old that they have been caught up in mountain-building activities, cooked at great depths, twisted out of all recognition, and then worn flat. The result is known as a metamorphic rock. Fossils tend to be destroyed in this process, but even when the Pre-Cambrian rocks are unaltered there are few fossils in them. There were not any hard shells or skeletons in Pre-Cambrian animals, so they did not fossilize well. The best Pre-Cambrian fossils were found at Ediacara in southern Australia. The rocks from here date from about 600 million years ago – at the very end of the Pre-Cambrian, and almost the beginning of the Cambrian, periods.

**Left:** The fossils of soft-bodied Pre-Cambrian creatures found at Ediacara in Australia, include (from top to bottom): circular types that were probably jellyfish; segmented animals, both flat and elongated, that must have been worms; and feather-shaped creatures that would have grown attached to the bottom of the sea bed, like modern sea pens. An assemblage of fossils, as shown here, gives a picture of how the ancient environment probably appeared.

# AGE OF MYSTERY

For most of Pre-Cambrian time the air was poisonous and the land was barren. There was not any oxygen in the atmosphere, and therefore nothing could exist on the early continents. Things could only live in the sea.

Microscopic plants – those that consist of only a single cell and give pond water its greenish tinge – evolved quite early. They could live by using the energy of sunlight to make food from the chemicals in the sea water around them. They gave off oxygen as a by-product of this action. The oxygen became dissolved in the sea water or bubbled to the surface, and gradually the oxygen levels built up in the atmosphere.

The earliest fossils are the remains of these tiny plants. In some areas today, the single-celled plants stick together and form mats on the sea floor. Mud sticks to these mats,

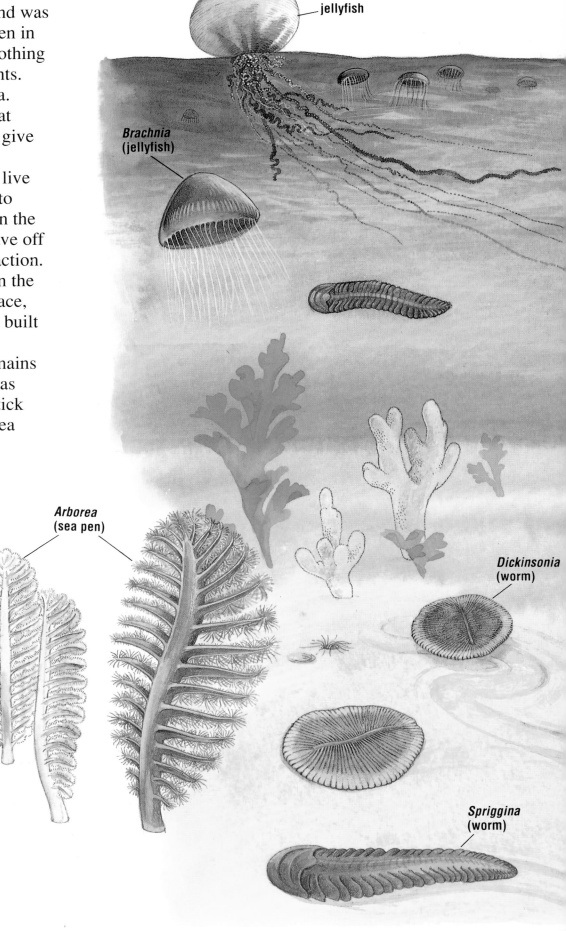

jellyfish

*Brachnia* (jellyfish)

*Arborea* (sea pen)

*Dickinsonia* (worm)

*Spriggina* (worm)

**Right:** The soft-bodied animals of the late Pre-Cambrian period, 600 million years ago, included worms, such as elongated *Spriggina* and disc-shaped *Dickinsonia*, feathery sea pens like *Arborea*, and jellyfish such as bell-shaped *Brachnia* and plate-like *Eoporpita*, as well as communal types that resembled the modern Portuguese man-of-war. This assemblage of creatures was found in Australia, but the same soft-bodied animals probably lived in shallow seas all over the world.

# PRE-CAMBRIAN

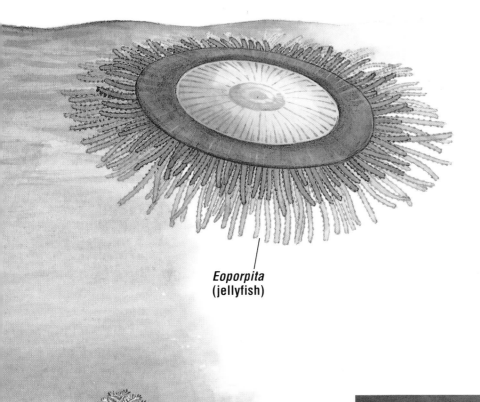

forming a layer, and then new plants grow on top of the mud attracting another mud layer. The result is a dome consisting of thin layers of mud, and called a stromatolite. Fossil stromatolites are known from Pre-Cambrian rocks 2,000 million years old.

By the end of the Pre-Cambrian period, much more complex creatures had developed. The remains of soft animals at Ediacara consist of worms, jellyfish, and the feather-like animals called sea pens. Ediacara is the best Pre-Cambrian fossil site, but the creatures found there must have lived in the seas throughout the world. Fossil sea pens are found in late Pre-Cambrian rocks in Canada and England as well.

*Eoporpita*
(jellyfish)

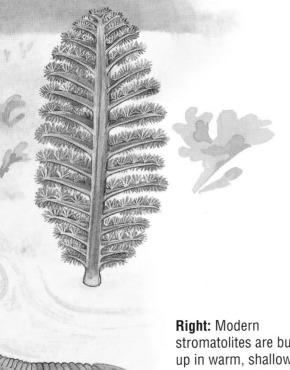

**Right:** Modern stromatolites are built up in warm, shallow waters where there are few animals to disturb the sediment of the sea bed. Pre-Cambrian stromatolites, looking just like the modern forms, are among the oldest, living things to be recognized in the fossil record.

# CAMBRIAN STORYBOOK

Around the Pre-Cambrian shield areas at the hearts of the continents lie old mountains of slightly younger rocks. To the eastern side of the Canadian Shield, lie the northern Appalachians. To the west, lie the Rockies. During Cambrian times, between 590 and 505 million years ago, the Canadian Shield was an island. The sands and muds that gathered in the coastal waters on each side were later turned into rock and crushed up against the shield area to form mountains. The same thing was happening to continents all over the world.

Cambrian rocks containing fossils are found in many places including Siberia, Scotland, North Africa, and the Antarctic Peninsula, but perhaps the best-known site is in the Rockies of British Columbia in Canada. Here, on a mountainside, is an outcrop of shale – a thin, flaky rock formed as layers of fine mud turned to stone. It is called the Burgess Shale and contains a remarkable collection of Cambrian fossils. It seems as if a whole sea bed full of living things had been engulfed by a flow of mud, and preserved. Many of the animals had soft bodies, like those of the late Pre-Cambrian, but most had skeletons and shells of some kind. Usually the skeleton of a jointed animal like a crab is only found fossilized in pieces, but there the burial was so quick that the most delicate feelers and whiskers are preserved.

From a highly detailed collection of fossils like this, we can deduce what the sea life was like all around the world at the time.

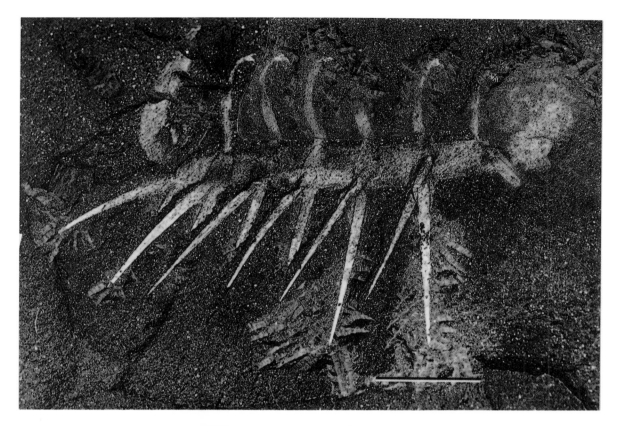

**Left:** Many of the strange creatures of the Burgess Shale became extinct soon after the Cambrian period and left no descendants. *Hallucigenia* is typical.

**Left:** The shales of the Burgess Formation on the Rocky Mountain slopes of British Columbia, in Canada, have yielded over 60,000 Cambrian fossils. Shale is a fine, sedimentary rock, formed from mud, and it splits easily into very thin sheets. Fossils were first seen in loose stones that had rolled down the slopes. In the detailed study that followed, blocks of shale from the original Burgess Formation outcrop were taken apart, bed by bed.

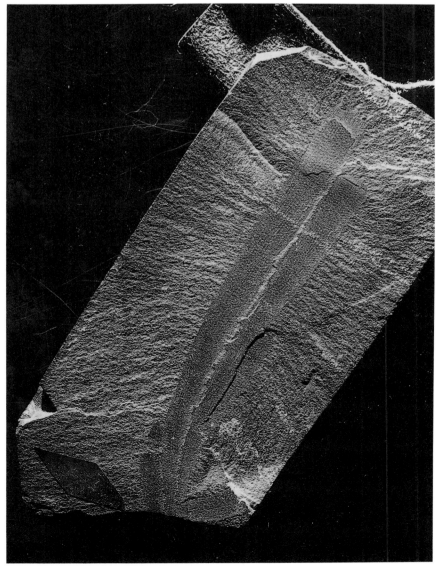

**Left:** The designs of some of the animals seemed to be very good. *Vauxia* is a representative of the sponge group that survived for a long time.

# THE FIRST GOOD FOSSILS

Suddenly, about 590 million years ago, animals developed hard shells. In Cambrian rocks, such as the Burgess Shale, we can see the first fossils of all different kinds of shelly animals. There were bivalves – our familiar seashells; gastropods – the snails and winkles; brachiopods – like the bivalves but unrelated; trilobites – jointed, many-legged animals related to the shrimps; corals – like sea anemones in cup-shaped shells; sponges – with skeletons made of masses of silica needles; and sea lilies – like braided starfish on stems. These were all totally unrelated animals, with quite different types of shells. It is possible that the build-up of oxygen in the sea water triggered the biological reactions that allowed hard shells to grow.

As well as these recognizable creatures, the Burgess Shale contains all sorts of things that have puzzled scientists ever since their discovery. What, for example, are we to make of the 1-inch long worm-like creature on stilt-like spines with jawed tentacles down its back and a scorpion-like tail? Or the 2-inch long spiny, slug-like animal with armor, like chain mail? It was almost as if evolution, having invented the hard skeleton, was trying out all kinds of new shapes and bodily forms just to see which would work best. By the end of the Cambrian era, most of these weird creatures had died out, and most of the major groups of animals that we know today had become established.

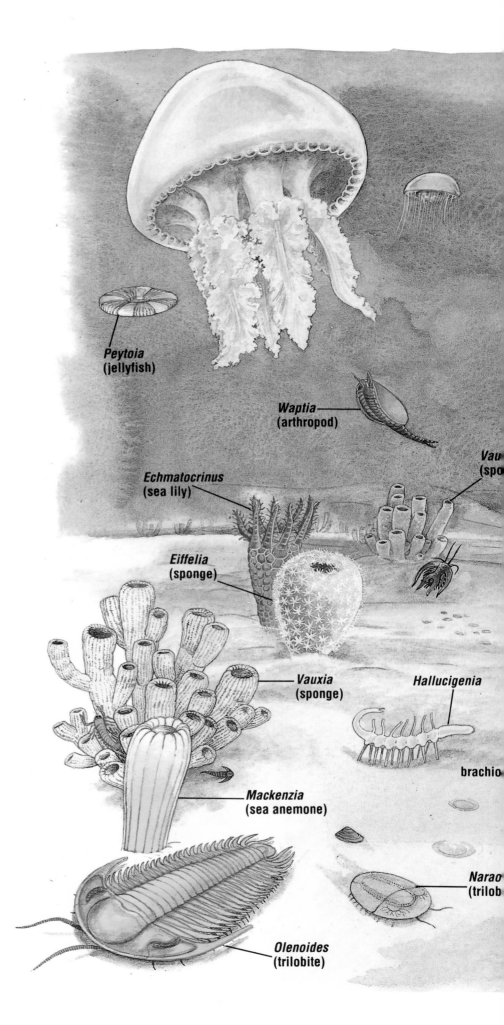

Peytoia
(jellyfish)

Waptia
(arthropod)

Vau
(spo

Echmatocrinus
(sea lily)

Eiffelia
(sponge)

Vauxia
(sponge)

Hallucigenia

Mackenzia
(sea anemone)

brachio

Narao
(trilob

Olenoides
(trilobite)

# CAMBRIAN

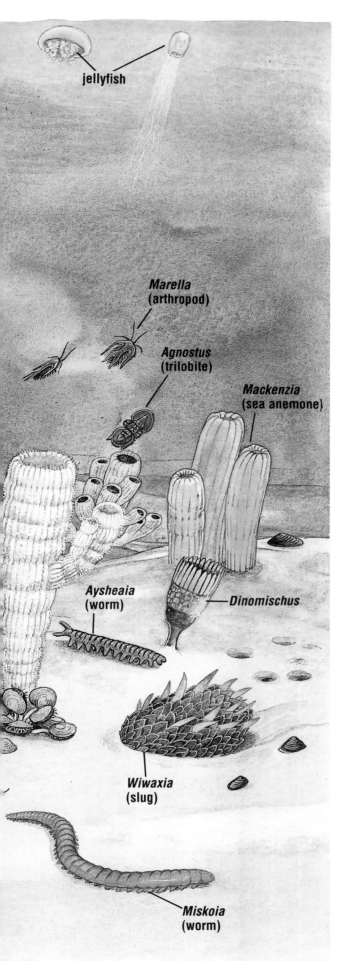

jellyfish

*Marella*
(arthropod)

*Agnostus*
(trilobite)

*Mackenzia*
(sea anemone)

*Aysheaia*
(worm)

*Dinomischus*

*Wiwaxia*
(slug)

*Miskoia*
(worm)

**Left:** On the Cambrian sea bed of British Columbia in Canada, sponges such as bulbous *Eiffelia* and branched *Vauxia*, the tubular sea anemone, *Mackenzia*, and the tentacled sea lily, *Echmatocrinus*, grew. The trilobites included the big *Olenoides*, the smaller *Naraoia*, and the swimming *Agnostus*, that was shaped like a figure-of-eight. Other swimming crustaceans included spiny *Marella*, the arthropod, *Waptia*, and the jellyfish, *Peytoia*, as well as various worms, such as *Aysheaia* and *Miskoia*, and also shellfish. The stilted, worm-like *Hallucigenia*, the egg-cup-shaped *Dinomischus*, and the armored slug, *Wiwaxia*, were very strange creatures with no modern descendants.

**Below:** Trilobites had head and tail shields, and a segmented body in between. They had a pair of feelers, two eyes, and many legs.

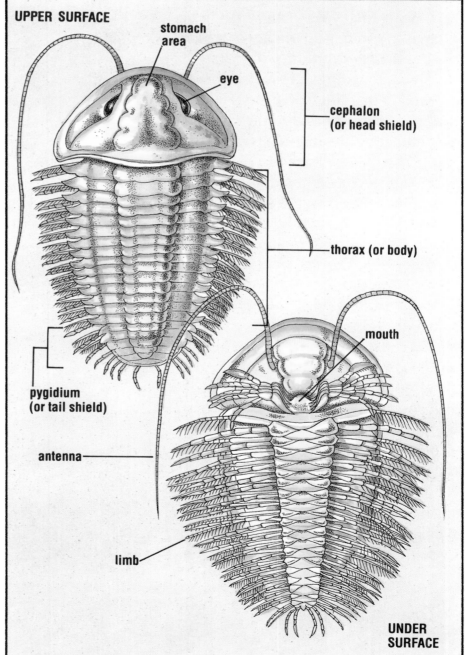

UPPER SURFACE

stomach area

eye

cephalon
(or head shield)

thorax (or body)

pygidium
(or tail shield)

mouth

antenna

limb

UNDER SURFACE

# ORDOVICIAN STORYBOOK

The next geological period, the Ordovician, lasted from 505 to 438 million years ago. During one part of the Ordovician period, the seas flooded across the edges of the continents, laying down mud and sand on top of the Pre-Cambrian shields and the beds of Cambrian rock that had already formed.

If we could see the Earth from space in those days, we would not be able to recognize any of the geography. The continents are constantly moving across the face of the Earth. They move at a rate of an inch or so each year – not much in a human lifetime. But when we think of the hundreds of millions of years involved in geological time, it is not surprising that the world looked quite different at any period in the past. The movement of the continents is often shown by the presence of volcanoes and the occurrence of earthquakes.

It was the same in the Ordovician period. The continent that is now North America and the one that is now northern Europe were moving toward one another. A chain of volcanic islands formed where Wales now lies. The Ordovician rocks of Wales consist of ancient lava flows. Deep ocean trenches lay offshore, like those of the Pacific Ocean close to the volcanic island chains. As a result, we see Ordovician deep-water shales in Scotland. These shales have fossils of the animals that drifted in the water far above them.

Elsewhere, particularly in the Appalachian Mountains, there are Ordovician shallow-water fossils.

**Above:** Ordovician rocks, that were formed in shallow water, contain fossils such as the shells of brachiopods and the stalks of sea lilies.

**Left**: *Lloydolithus* was one of the specialized trilobites of the time. Its lack of eyes indicates that it had lived on muddy sea beds.

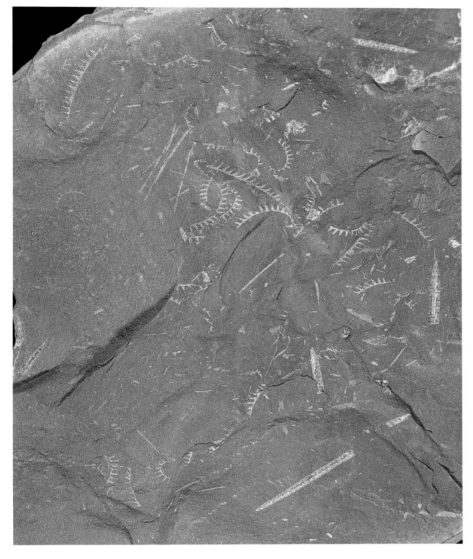

**Left and above:** Graptolite fossils lie in many types of Ordovician rock. They floated in the oceans and, when they were dead, sank to the bottom of the sea to become fossilized in whatever rocks were forming. Examples of these fossils include curved *Rastrites* (left), and two-branched *Didymograptus* (above).

**Left:** The little brachiopod, *Lingula,* survives unchanged to this day. Its living conditions must have remained the same.

# LIFE DIVERSIFIES

**M**any of the animal groups that evolved in the Cambrian period continued into Ordovician times. The trilobites, in particular, are common fossils of Ordovician rocks. These began to develop along different lines. Those that swam around in the sea were light and feathery, those that burrowed in the sand were spade-shaped, and so on.

An important group that developed at this time were the graptolites. Their fossils look like little hacksaw blades. Each tooth of the blade was a horny cup that held a tiny animal. When they were alive, they drifted in vast numbers in the surface waters of all the oceans of the world. When they died, they sank to the bottoms and were fossilized in the shales, sandstones, or limestones that were forming at the time. As a result we

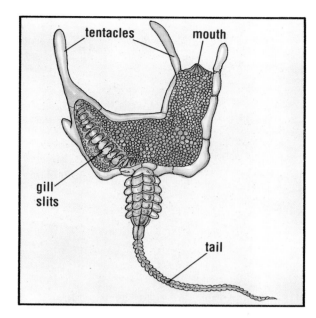

**Left:** The tadpole-like echinoderm, *Cothurnocystis,* may have been our ancestor. It pushed its way along the sea bed with its muscular tail, and fed itself by sweeping particles of food into its mouth with its tentacles. The illustration is about twice its natural size.

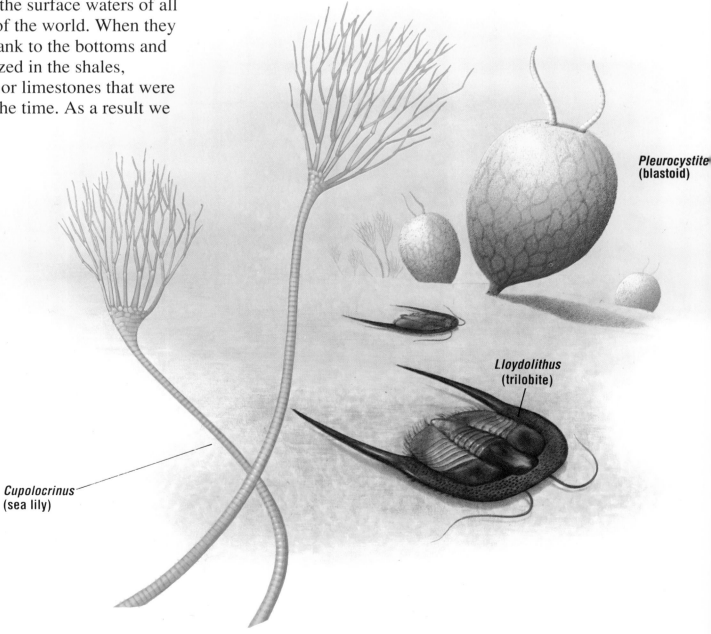

*Pleurocystite* (blastoid)

*Lloydolithus* (trilobite)

*Cupolocrinus* (sea lily)

**Right:** A graptolite was a communal animal, and it consisted of many individuals. Each animal was set in its own horny cup and was arranged along a branch; each animal would extend its feathery feeding organ into the water for food. As they evolved, graptolites tended to become simpler, and reduced the numbers of their branches.

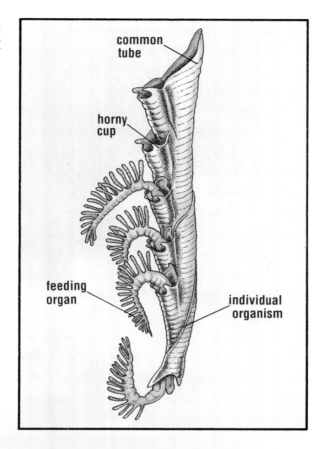

common tube

horny cup

feeding organ

individual organism

find graptolites in Ordovician rocks all over the world. We can also put an exact date on such a rock by seeing what kind of graptolite it contains, because the graptolite group evolved and changed very rapidly.

The echinoderms – the starfish, sea urchins, sea cucumbers, and sea lilies – were another important Ordovician group. One member looked something like a flattened sea lily, but it must have pushed itself along on the sea bed with its muscular stem that had become a tail, with its tentacles and mouth pointing forward. Later on, the descendants of this creature developed a backbone and gave rise to the first fish, which in turn eventually evolved into the higher vertebrates.

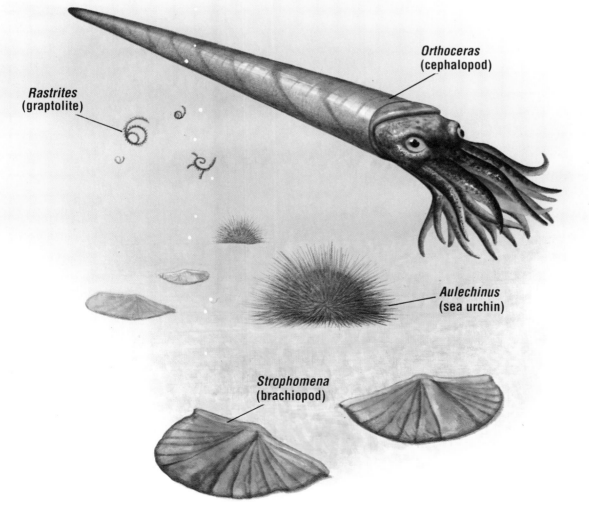

*Rastrites* (graptolite)

*Orthoceras* (cephalopod)

*Aulechinus* (sea urchin)

*Strophomena* (brachiopod)

**Left:** Life on the Ordovician sea bed was abundant. Trilobites, such as *Lloydolithus*, crawled among the shelled brachiopods, like *Strophomena*, and echinoderms such as the graceful sea lily, *Cupolocrinus*, the bulbous blastoid, *Pleurocystites*, and the sea urchin, *Aulechinus*. The graptolites, such as *Rastrites*, and the shelled and tentacled cephalopod, *Orthoceras*, floated above them.

21

# SILURIAN STORYBOOK

At the end of the Ordovician period there was an ice age. Areas of continents that were near the poles were covered in ice. As the Silurian period began, this ice was melting away once more. We can tell all this because glaciers always scrape up masses of clay and boulders, carry them along, and dump them when they melt. There are rocks made of this glacial debris, dating from Silurian times, in Argentina and Bolivia.

The seas spread over the continents again during the Silurian period. We do not get many sandstones or shales among the Silurian rocks. It seems that so much of the land was covered that there was little mud or sand being washed into the sea. Instead, most of the shallow water rocks are

**Right:** The limestone in Wenlock, near the border between England and Wales, is typical of the shallow-water rocks that were formed in the Silurian period. Such little sediment was deposited, that the skeletons of all the animals that lived there, piled up on the sea bed, and eventually they formed the rock itself. Brachiopod shells and disc-shaped sections of crinoid stems are shown in this picture.

limestones – the kind of rocks that form in clear water. Many of the limestones are reef limestones. These indicate clear water in which so many creatures – bivalves, corals, sea lilies, and so on – were living that they all grew on top of the empty shells and skeletons of the creatures that had gone before. The rock that then formed consists of nothing but a mass of fossils.

On land, things were beginning to change. The fossils of the first land plants are known from this time. These grew along the shores of lakes and would have evolved from water plants left high and dry. The best fossils are a result of these plants having been petrified by the mineral silica as silica-rich waters from hot springs and volcanoes engulfed the struggling greenery.

**Below:** The first plants to grow in the air in Silurian times were very simple – a stalk with a fruiting body, that sprouted above the surface of the water.

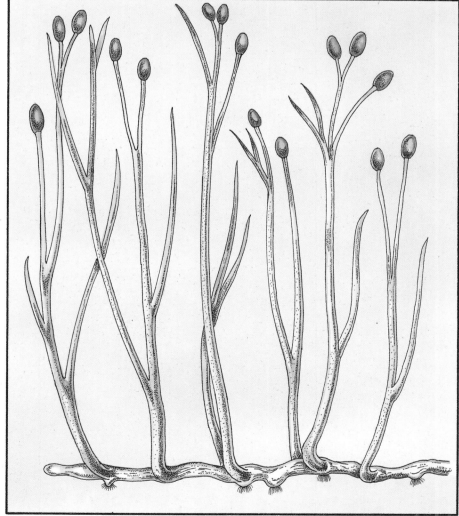

# THE TIME OF FIRST LAND LIFE

The warm shallow waters of the Silurian seas must have been full of life. The sea bed would have been covered in crushed and broken shells in which sea lilies and corals were anchored. Most of the corals were not like today's branching reef-building corals, in which thousands of individuals are joined together to make a huge mass of shelly skeleton. The corals of these times were more like today's sea anemones but covered in a horn-shaped shell. Cephalopods – the animal group to which the modern octopus and squid belong – swam through these waters hunting shellfish. Unlike today's forms, these cephalopods were not soft and naked, but had strong chambered shells which are often found as fossils.

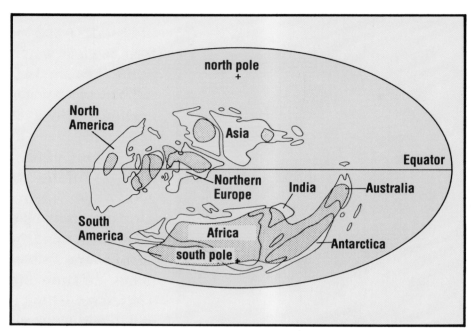

**Above:** The Silurian continents were in different positions from the continents of today.

**Right:** The clear waters of the Silurian seas supported reefs built by many different kinds of organisms, including the spherical alga, *Ischadites*, and the brachiopod, *Stricklandia*. Corals, such as chain-like *Halysites*, and thick beds of sea lilies, such as *Gissocrinus*, filtered food from the water, while the trilobites, such as this *Dalmanites*, still crawled on the limy sand.

*Halysites* (coral)

# SILURIAN

The first fish lived in the Silurian seas, but these were primitive. They did not have jaws – just sucker-shaped mouths like modern lampreys.

On land, things were changing. As before there were deserts everywhere. The landscape was an unrelieved wilderness of bleak, bare rocks and stony wastes. But now, for the first time, there were tinges of green along the beaches and the edges of rivers and lakes. Primitive plants that could survive out of the water – nothing more than a stem and a primitive leaf – had developed. Once the first few had lived and died on the shoreline, their remains broke down and began to fertilize the soil. This made it easier for others to grow. The colonization of land had begun.

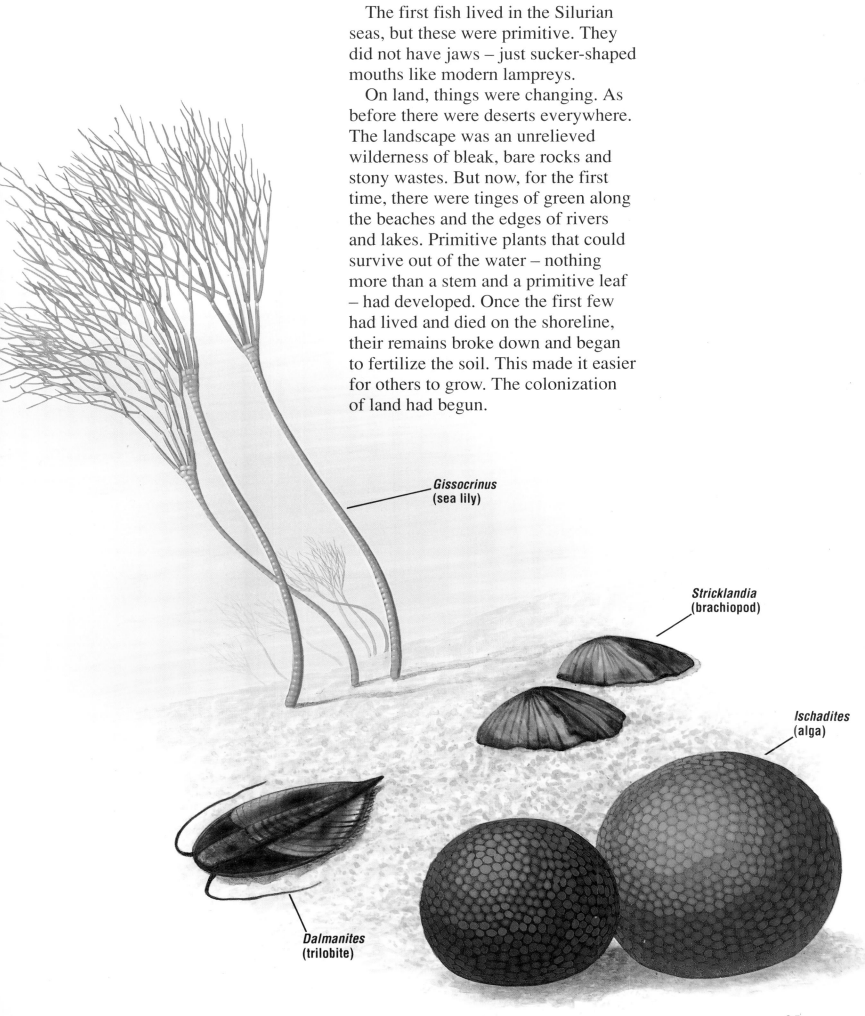

*Gissocrinus*
(sea lily)

*Stricklandia*
(brachiopod)

*Ischadites*
(alga)

*Dalmanites*
(trilobite)

# DEVONIAN STORYBOOK

A dramatic thing happened to some of the main continents in Devonian times, 408 to 360 million years ago. The continent that is now North America, and that which is now northern Europe, collided with one another. As they did so the Cambrian, Ordovician, and Silurian rocks that had been forming in the sea area between them became pushed up into a vast mountain range. The same thing happened relatively recently – in the last 50 million years –when the continent of India collided with that of Asia and the mountain range of The Himalayas buckled up between the two. The Devonian mountain range which was formed between what is now North America and northern Europe was every bit as big as The Himalayas.

Rivers pouring off the mountains spread their deposits on the surrounding dry plains. The most distinctive Devonian rocks are sandstones that formed in deserts, in which we can see beds of rock that

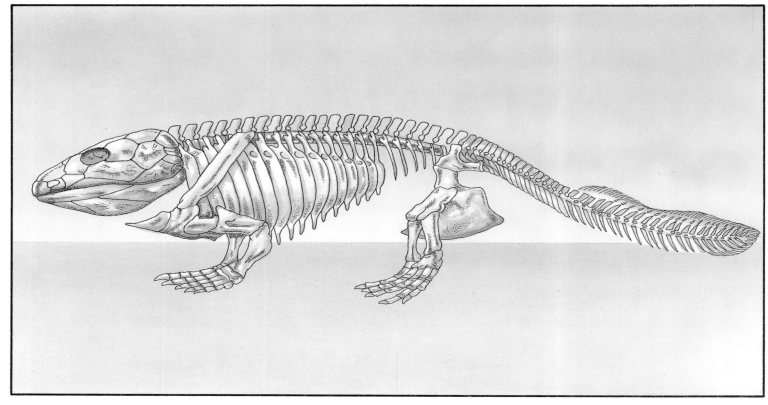

must have been laid down by river currents. A river current produces a characteristic S-shaped curve in the cross section of the bed. There are many lake deposits as well, and these contain the fossils of many different kinds of fish. Occasionally, there are fossils of land plants, too, and of the earliest land animals. The Devonian rocks of the Appalachians, Greenland, and Spitzbergen are important for their fossils of early land life.

And, where is the Devonian mountain range now? Most of it is worn away, but we can still see the stumps of it in the Appalachians, the Scottish Highlands, and the mountains of Norway.

**Left:** The strongly-bedded, red sandstones of northern Scotland, and the Orkney Islands off its north coast, were laid down in inland lakes, streams, and deserts in the Devonian times.

**Left**: One of the earliest amphibians, the *Ichthyostega,* from the Devonian period of Greenland, had powerful five-toed limbs, anchored to strong, bony girdles. Its ribs overlapped to protect its soft insides. These are features of a land animal. However, it still had the skull and the tail of a fish, and it must have spent much of its time swimming.

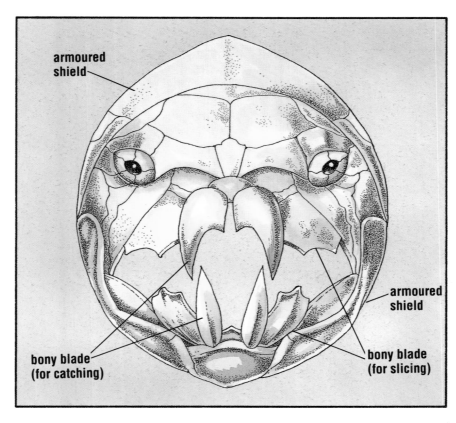

armoured shield

bony blade (for catching)

armoured shield

bony blade (for slicing)

**Left:** Among the many fish fossils of the Devonian marine rocks, probably the most spectacular was *Dunkleostus.* The skull was over 2 feet long and heavily armored, and it was jointed to a sheath of armor that covered the front half of its body. The sharply-pointed armored plates, that took the place of teeth at the front of its mouth, show that it was a fierce hunter.

# AGE OF FISH

The water life of Devonian times was as varied as it had been in previous periods. Corals and sea lilies flourished in the shallow seas, but the trilobites and graptolites that had been so important in the Ordovician and Silurian times were declining now.

It was in the rivers, the estuaries, and the shallow lakes that the most exciting water life was to be found. The primitive jawless fish of the Silurian had now developed in many different directions.

One of the first fish groups to develop was the shark group. These had a skeleton that was made of gristle rather than of bone, and some of the Devonian types looked very similar to today's sharks.

A peculiar group of armored fish called the placoderms made a brief appearance in the Devonian. These had armored heads and bodies and, usually, long, rat-like tails. Some were huge, with *Dunkleostus* measuring 11 feet and 6 inches long.

The bony fishes were the most successful and have continued until today. In Devonian times, they branched into two groups – the ray-fins and the lobe-fins. The former had fins that were supported by narrow rays of bone, as in most modern fish. The latter had fins supported by muscular lobes, and they could pull themselves along with them if they were ever stranded on dry land. They also had lungs that could enable them to breathe while out of the water. The first land-living vertebrates developed from these fish .

**Right:** We can see how the hunting fish, *Dunkleostus*, appeared in real life, by the arrangement of its armor and bones. It was as long as some of the big sharks of today. Its armor was confined to its front quarters, so that its eel-like tail was flexible enough to drive it quickly through the water, and its fins had enough give to control its movements. The marks of the muscles on the inside of its armor indicate that it had a powerful bite. *Dunkleostus* must have been the terror of the Devonian seas.

**Left:** Among the other Devonian fish of the seas and rivers were *Moythomasia* (top), a primitive relative of the ray-finned fish of today, the lobe-finned *Dipnorhynchus* (center), with lungs and pairs of limbs that was the origin of amphibians, and *Gemuendina* (bottom), a skate-like type of armored placoderm, that fed off the sea bed.

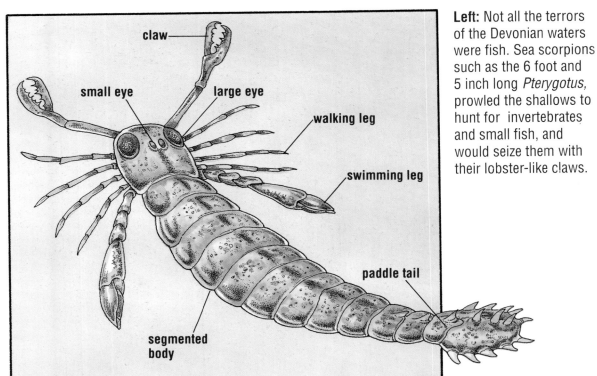

claw

small eye        large eye

walking leg

swimming leg

paddle tail

segmented body

**Left:** Not all the terrors of the Devonian waters were fish. Sea scorpions such as the 6 foot and 5 inch long *Pterygotus,* prowled the shallows to hunt for invertebrates and small fish, and would seize them with their lobster-like claws.

# THE FIRST FORESTS

The land was turning green in Devonian times. Wherever there was enough moisture – along river banks or by lake sides – plants gained a root hold. The plants of the time were quite primitive – nothing more advanced than today's ferns – but some of them had developed sturdy trunks and grew into quite respectable trees. The first forests were present by the end of the period. The simple plants of the Silurian period were still there, but, besides the ferns, the main plants were the club mosses. Today, these club mosses are insignificant. They are little plants consisting of a bunch of branches no longer than your fingers and covered with scale-like leaves. By Devonian times, they had grown to tree size.

The backboned animals left the

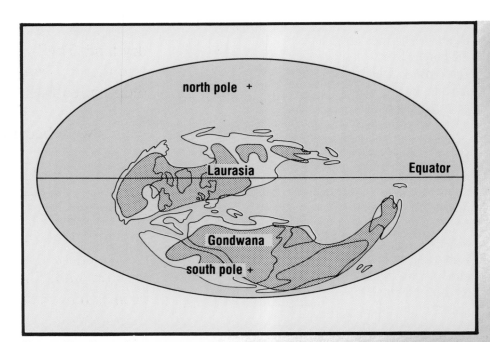

**Above:** The Devonian continents had begun to move together, and so new mountain ranges were produced.

**Right:** Along the edges of the rivers that poured off the newly formed Devonian mountain ranges, the first forests gained their foot hold. Tall trees, related to modern club mosses, thrust their droopy branches up through ferns, growing below. Insects and millipedes crawled through this new undergrowth, and these were pursued by the first amphibians, such as the 40-inch-long *Ichthyostega*.

water at this time and colonized the
dry land. The lobe-finned fish could
pull themselves over the ground on
their paired fins and breathe the air.
They may have done this because the
waters were becoming dangerous with
all the other fish present, or to chase
and eat the insects and spiders that
had developed at the same time as the
first land plants. From these fish
developed the first amphibians –
animals that could spend most of their
time on land. The earliest known,
such as *Ichthyostega*, and its relative,
*Acanthostega*, from Greenland, still
had fish-like skulls and fish-like fins
on their tails.

These fossils are found now in very
cold places, but in Devonian times
places like Greenland and Spitzbergen
lay on the Equator.

# MISSISSIPPIAN STORYBOOK

The Carboniferous period, from 360 to 286 million years ago, is such an important one that geologists have divided it into two separate periods – the Mississippian and the Pennsylvanian. These two periods are known by geologists outside the United States as the Lower and Upper Carboniferous periods respectively. The cut-off point between the two is 320 million years ago.

During the Mississippian, or Lower Carboniferous, shallow seas flooded the low-lying lands once more. Much of North America and Europe became covered with water. Limestones again became the most important rocks produced at the time, and thick limestones dating from Mississippian times can be seen in many parts of the world. The massive Redwall limestone, the thick bed of rock that produces the vertical cliffs in the Grand Canyon, was laid down at this time, as was the limestone forming the Pennine Hills of central England.

Common fossils of the time are sea lilies, corals, bivalves, and brachiopods. The brachiopods look something like the bivalves, in that the living creature is encased in two shells. However, they are not related. Bivalves and brachiopods have developed similar forms because they have adapted to live in the same way under similar conditions. We call this phenomenon convergent evolution, and it crops up time after time in the fossil record.

Sharks and other fish are also common Mississippian fossils.

**Above:** Massive beds of limestone, such as these in Cheddar Gorge in Somerset, England, were formed in the shallow seas of the Mississippian period.

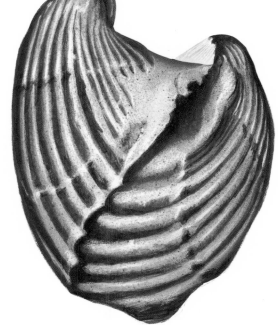

**Right:** A brachiopod (shown here), was common in the Mississippian seas, but differed from a bivalve shellfish in that its two shells were unequal. In a bivalve, the shells are mirror images of each other and are equal.

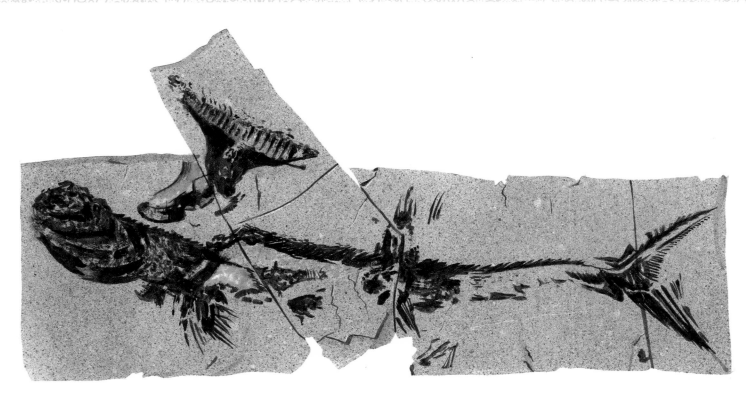

**Above:** Shark skeletons are often found in marine rocks of Mississippian times. The remains of this *Stethacanthus* show a toothy structure all along its back fin.

**Above:** Most Mississippian corals lived in cup-shaped shells, with a radiating pattern of internal walls that supported the lining of its stomach.

**Left:** Complete sea-lily fossils show its cup-shaped body, the ring of tentacles around its mouth, and the stalk that anchored it to the bed of the sea.

# THE LIMY SEAS

The clear Mississippian seas around the world supported a great deal of animal life. The tentacles of the waving groves of sea lilies extracted food particles from the water. Between their stems lived the many types of shellfish – bivalve and brachiopod – and the cup-like corals. Through the waters myriad kinds of fish swam. Most ate the small creatures that swam around, some nibbled the seaweeds, but others, shark-like, chased the shoals of fish and ate whatever they could catch.

Toward the edges of the shallow seas, the water became muddier as sand and silt were washed in from the surrounding mountains. The fish tended to be fossilized in the sandstones and shales formed here, rather than in the limestones found in clearer water further out to sea.

On land, the forests continued to grow and flourish, and amphibians developed into all sorts of shapes and sizes – small ones that chased insects through the undergrowth, and huge crocodile-like forms that swam in the shallow streams eating others of their own kind. If the amphibians were not perfectly adapted to land life, it was because they went through a tadpole stage when young and always had to come back to the water to lay their eggs when adult.

During the Mississippian period, a new kind of creature developed – one that could lay a hard-shelled egg on land. Such a creature did not need to spend any part of its life in the water. It was a fully land-living animal – the first reptile.

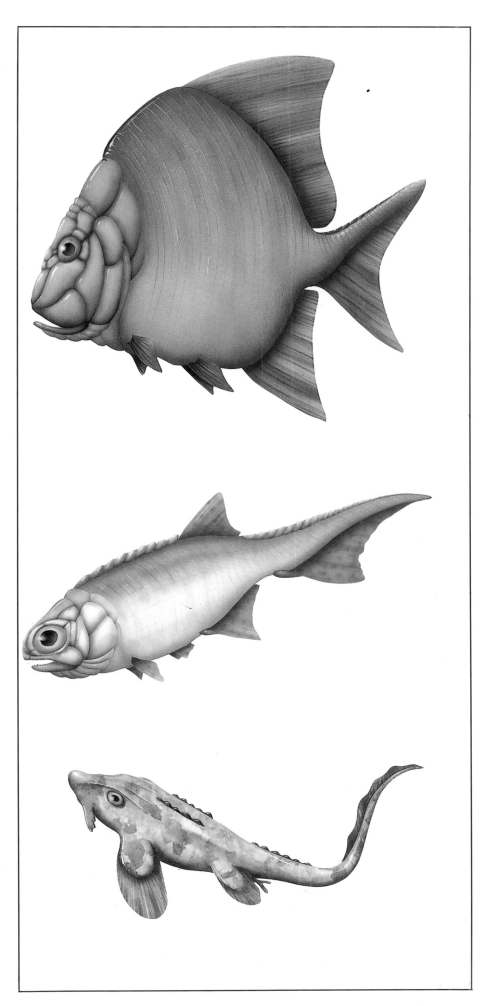

**Right:** The shallow seas of the Mississippian period teemed with fish. *Platystomus* (top) was an early, ray-finned, bony fish with a very flattened body. Its relative, *Canobius* (center) was more cylindrical, but both probably fed on tiny, floating bits of food. *Deltoptychius* (bottom) had a skeleton of cartilage and was a shellfish-eater, like the modern ratfish.

**Left:** One of the many sharks of the Mississippian period was *Stethacanthus*. It was a strange creature because it had an anvil-shaped, dorsal fin that was covered with teeth, and many teeth were on its head as well. We do not know why these structures were there, but the vast array of teeth probably were used for frightening enemies away.

# PENNSYLVANIAN STORYBOOK

As the shallow seas of the Mississippian period lay across the continents, the mountain ranges thrown up in the preceding Devonian period were crumbling and eroding away. This erosion continued into the Pennsylvanian period, and the geography changed a great deal. Rivers and streams brought down masses of sand and silt, and these were deposited as deltas and mud banks in the shallow seas. Whole areas of the sea were built up above sea level and became thickly forested swamps.

Occasionally the sea flooded back and drowned the forests, then the process would start again. First there would be mud flowing in from the distant land. Then, as the deltas came closer, there would be a deposit of

**Above:** The thick beds of coal, on which the industry of the last two centuries was based, were laid down in the Pennsylvanian period.

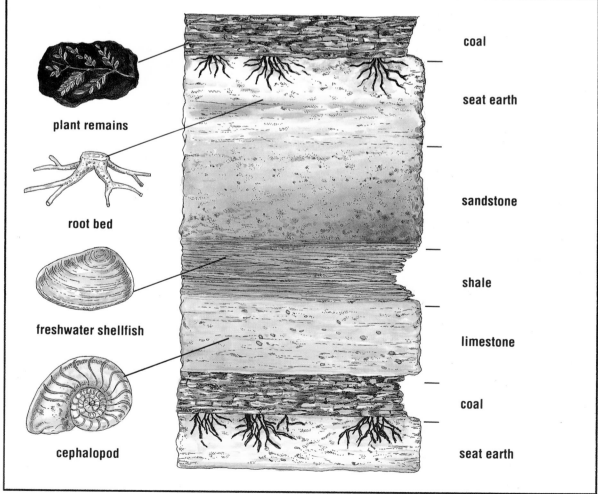

plant remains

root bed

freshwater shellfish

cephalopod

coal

seat earth

sandstone

shale

limestone

coal

seat earth

**Left:** A sequence of Pennsylvanian rocks often contains successive beds of shale, sandstone, fireclay or seat earth (that is, a pale sandstone with root remains), and coal. These layers reflect the changing environments during this period, as swamps and deltas were built up out of the water and dried out.

**Below:** *Annularia,* a relative of the modern horsetails, had rosettes of leaves along its stalk.

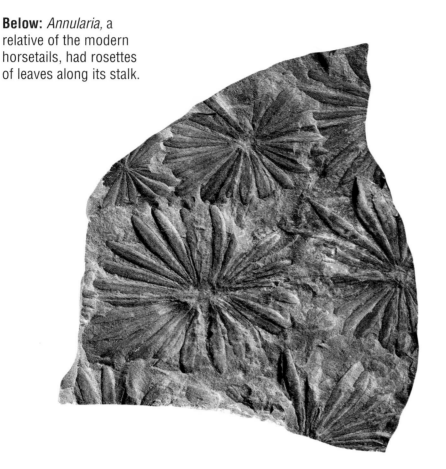

sand. When the sand was built up above sea level the forest would grow. Then it would be drowned once more.

The result of all this is a sequence of rocks which starts with a bed of limestone. This has a bed of shale above it, then a bed of sandstone, then a bed of compressed carbon from the vegetation, then another bed of limestone. Often the limestone is missing, perhaps because the forest was flooded by a river rather than the sea. Pennsylvanian rocks are made up of many thousands of such cycles.

The beds of carbon are important to us. Compressed vegetable matter like this is coal. When these Pennsylvanian beds are thick enough, they represent the coal seams that are worked around the world.

**Left:** Huge tree roots and underground stalks are fossilized in the sandstones beneath the coal beds sometimes, as shown here in Glasgow, Scotland.

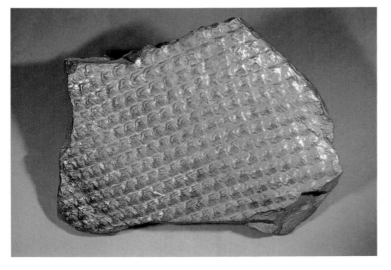

**Left:** The diamond pattern on the fossil bark of the club-moss tree, *Lepidodendron,* shows where the long, strap-like leaves were once attached.

**Above:** The ribbed, segmented trunk of the fossil, *Calamites,* shows that it was a giant horsetail at one time.

# THE COAL AGE

The vast, dank swamps, the steaming deltas, and the gloomy forests of the Pennsylvanian period must have been strange silent places.

We would hardly have recognized the plants that lived there. Along the edges of the sluggish streams and the stagnant bogs, in the murky water itself, there grew deep "reed-beds" of horsetails. These were not the brittle knee-high horsetails that we know today, but huge woody types, some looking like pale Christmas trees that grew to heights of 33 feet or so. Club-moss trees grew in shallower water and the soft mud of the banks. These were anchored in the sticky peat by a flat network of branching roots while the straight, woody, ribbed trunks towered 100 feet or more to

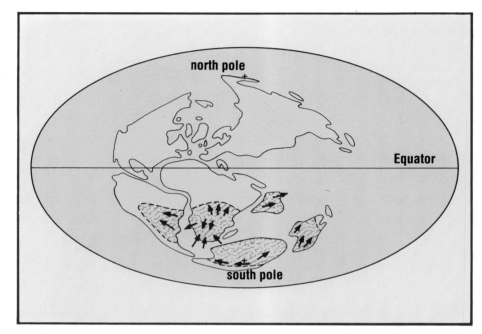

**Above:** Coal swamps developed around the new mountain ranges in Pennsylvanian times.

**Above:** The oldest reptile was found in 1989 in Mississippian rocks, in Scotland. It has not been named yet but some scientists are calling it *Lizzie.*

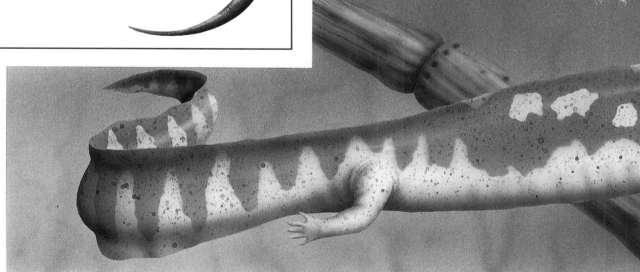

their crowns of strap-like leaves. On drier ground, there were trees of a group called the cordaites that were distant ancestors of the conifers. Everywhere was an undergrowth of ferns and creeping horsetails.

No birds sang in the green gloom. The only noises would have been the hum of giant insects, for there were dragonfly-like insects the size of parrots, and the occasional splash as a giant amphibian slid, alligator-like, into the black water. In the stench of rotting wood and leaves, millipedes 6 feet long heaved around digesting whatever goodness the fungi and bacteria left behind, while in the hollow stumps of the club-moss trees, early reptiles laid their hard-shelled eggs.

Ice covered the continents around the South Pole at the end of this period.

**Left:** The steaming swamps of the Pennsylvanian lowlands supported thickets of giant horsetails, jungles of ferns, and very dense forests of club-moss trees. The murky waters were full of fish, such as *Cornuboniscus,* and these fish were chased by amphibians, such as the very large, 15-foot-long *Eogyrinus.*

# PERMIAN STORYBOOK

Throughout time the continents moved. In the Devonian period, North America collided with northern Europe and threw up a mountain range between. In the Pennsylvanian period, a huge landmass consisting of most of the continents of the southern hemisphere collided with this combined continent and produced another mountain range. Then, in the Permian period – 286 to 248 million years ago – the eastern edge of Europe collided with the mainland of Asia. The mountain range so produced is still with us in the form of the Urals. As a result, just about all the continents of the globe happened to become fused together to form a single vast supercontinent that geologists call Pangea.

Climates changed as well. Pangea was so immense that most of it was a long way from the sea. As a result, only dry winds blew across it. The interior was one vast desert. We can deduce this from the rocks that were formed at the time. Many places have thick beds of Permian sandstone. Through a microscope we can see that the sand grains are rounded, just like those in a modern desert. In addition, we can see the shapes of the original sand dunes preserved in the rock. These result in S-shaped beds, something like those formed by river currents, but much bigger.

The beginning of the period saw an ice age as well. We can find ice-deposited Permian rocks in South America, southern Africa, Australia, Antarctica, and India. At that time these continents were all together and situated near the South Pole.

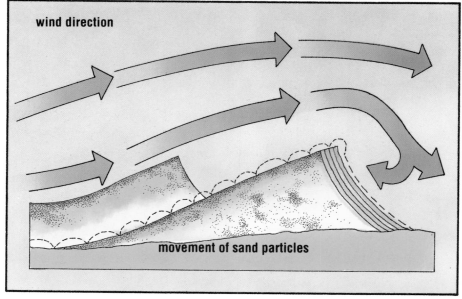

wind direction

movement of sand particles

**Left:** The huge sweeps of curved bedding in the red sandstones, found in western England, show that they were formed from desert sand dunes.

**Below:** Skeletons of very advanced reptiles have been found in the desert sandstones of Pangea. *Thrinaxodon,* from South Africa, had a skeleton very much similar to a mammal's skeleton. The mammals themselves evolved from such reptiles.

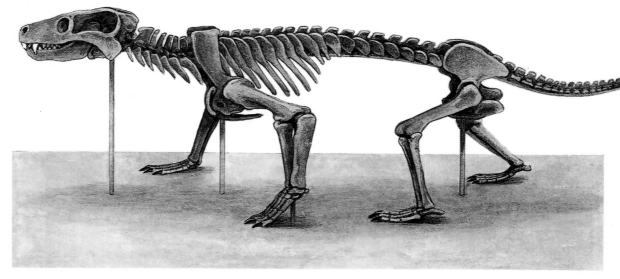

**Below:** The mammal-like reptiles evolved from more conventional types. *Dimetrodon* was like a large lizard, but it also had a row of tall spines along the middle of its back.

**Left:** Sand dunes move as wind blows the sand particles up the windward slope and deposits them down the leeward slope. This produces a curved, layered effect, that appears in the sandstone resulting from this movement.

# A TIME OF DESERTS

The prevailing dry climate of the Permian period produced a change in the plant and animal life.

Plants that were better able to withstand dry conditions spread over most of the continent. The main type of plant was a kind of a fern that reproduced by seed – something we do not see any more.

The amphibians adapted quite well to the new conditions. Enormous armored, land-living types evolved. *Eryops* was about 6 feet long and was as squat as a pig. *Peltobatrachus* was smaller, about 2 feet long, but armored like an armadillo. Three-foot-long *Platyhystrix* had a sail on its back like some of the reptiles of the time.

These still needed the water in which to breed, so it is not surprising that it was the reptiles that developed best in the new drier landscapes. One of the most important groups of the Permian started off by developing sails on their backs. These could keep their bodies cool or warm, by using the sails as heat radiators or solar collectors. *Dimetrodon* was the best-known of these. Later in the Permian, they became more efficient at regulating their heat and became "warm-blooded" like modern mammals. They also became hairy and walked the way mammals do. This group is known as the mammal-like reptiles, and eventually evolved into the mammals themselves.

Another important reptile group, called the thecodonts, were more crocodile-like. They spent much of their time in what water they could find, while the mammal-like reptiles were the masters of the land.

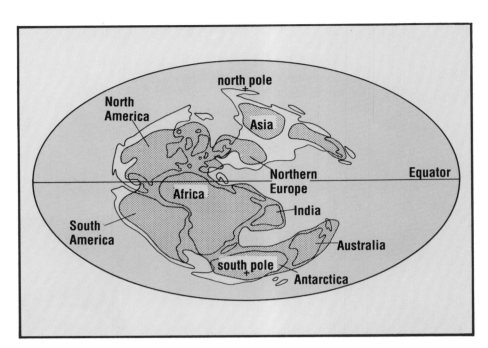

**Above:** The Permian landmasses had almost all come together as one great continent.

# PERMIAN

**Below:** The Permian landscape of North America had many arid plains. The Carboniferous swamps had died back to a few damp areas around the foothills of the mountains. The big amphibians had practically all died, and reptiles, such as the sail-backed *Dimetrodon,* started to appear. It was a meat-eater that could regulate its temperature, by holding its sail to the sun or the wind.

**Above:** In the late Permian period, reptiles, such as *Lycaenops,* began to look very much like mammals, because they had straight legs and teeth of different sizes.

# TRIASSIC STORYBOOK

The single supercontinent of Pangea still covered one-third of the globe in the Triassic, 248 to 213 million years ago. The same dry winds blew across it as in the Permian, and the desert conditions still prevailed. The rest of the world was covered by a single super ocean that geologists call Panthalassa.

The huge mountain ranges built in the preceding periods were now beginning to wear down to more rounded hills. Where they were close to the sea, these hills caught the rain from the sea winds, and rivers flowed down to the plains. Forested swamps grew at the edge of the deserts. In Arizona, there is a region called the Petrified Forest. A mass of fossilized Triassic logs and tree-trunks lies there. The site seems to represent a fossil log-jam, where Triassic floodwaters washed tree trunks downstream until they were caught in the river narrows and buried.

Close by in New Mexico, scientists found a mass of skeletons of small two-footed dinosaurs dating from about this time. The dinosaurs were meat-eaters, as we can tell by the teeth, and one of them had the bones of a young dinosaur inside it.

Elsewhere in Triassic rocks we find many bird-like footprints. These trace fossils also belong to small dinosaurs, and they can tell us how the dinosaurs hunted in packs, and where they lived.

All this evidence, from many different sites, can be put together to give us a picture of land life in the Triassic period.

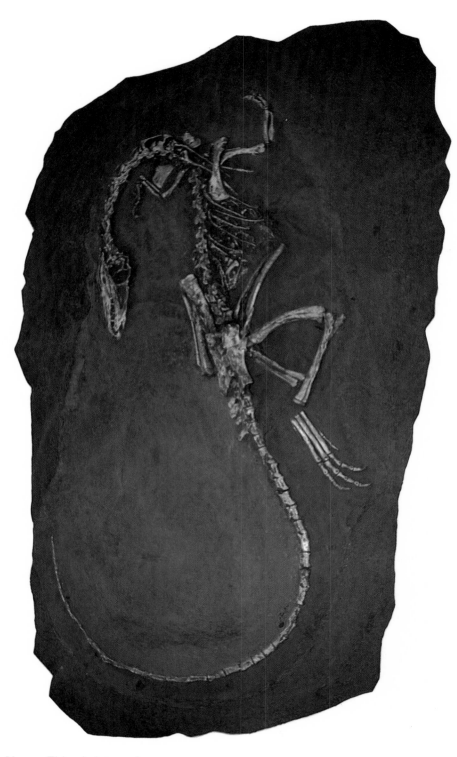

**Above:** This skeleton of the lightly-built dinosaur, *Coelophysis,* was one of about twelve discovered in the middle Triassic rocks at Ghost Ranch in New Mexico. The little bones in the stomach area are those of a young dinosaur.

**Right:** Footprints in the widespread, Triassic, desert sandstones, like this three-toed example from Connecticut, show that small dinosaurs, like *Coelophysis,* moved around in packs and family groups.

**Above:** Fossilized tree trunks lie on the desert floor in the Petrified Forest in Arizona. They are the remains of conifers, that were buried by floodwaters in the Triassic period.

# THE RISE OF THE DINOSAURS

Using the fossil evidence that has been unearthed in places like North America, we can look into the world of the Triassic dinosaurs.

Through a forest of conifers and ferns, on a fertile patch between the hills and the desert, there hunts a pack of about a dozen small dinosaurs. The dinosaur is *Coelophysis*, one of the first of the dinosaur meat-eaters. The largest is about 10 feet long, but most are smaller. They leave the shadow of the monkey puzzle trees and walk across a mud bank, leaving their bird-like footprints as they go. It is a bad day – there is not much food around. Finally, overcome by hunger, the largest seizes one of the youngsters in the pack and eats it. Eventually, however, they all succumb to hunger, and they all die

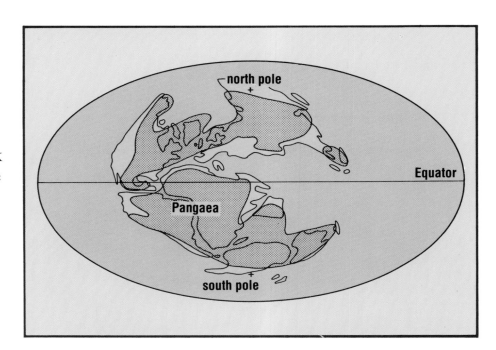

**Above:** All the continents were fused together to form one, huge super continent, in the Triassic period.

**Above:** Rat-like *Haramaia* was typical of the early mammals that evolved during the Triassic period.

and are fossilized in the same spot.

*Coelophysis*, and the other early dinosaurs, evolved from crocodile-like thecodonts that kept to the water in Permian times. Once the mammal-like reptiles had died out, the thecodonts spread over the land. Their long swimming hind legs and their strong paddling tail allowed them to walk balanced on two legs. The basic dinosaur shape developed.

The first mammals also appeared in the Triassic period. They were able to adjust their body temperature – a state we call "warm-blooded" – to allow them to live in hot and cold conditions. A furry coat helped them to do this. They bore their young alive, and did not need to lay eggs. One of the earliest well-known mammals was small, rat-like *Haramaia*.

**Left:** Forests of trees, similar to redwoods, spread across the foothills of southern North America, and lined the banks of the streams, that washed down from the new mountains. Packs of small dinosaurs, like *Coelophysis,* hunted here, and they left their tracks and their bones in the sediments of the rivers. They probably hunted the other reptiles of the time, as well as the mammals that had newly evolved.

# EARLY JURASSIC STORYBOOK

**A**t the beginning of the Jurassic period, which lasted from 213 to 144 million years ago, the shallow seas returned to the continental area. There was still the one big super continent of Pangea, but the edges were being washed by the ocean.

As a result there are many shales and limestones – rocks laid down in the sea – dating from Jurassic times. The fossils in these show that the sea life had changed since the earlier times. Gone were the trilobites and graptolites, and the shellfish and corals were much more like those of today. Everywhere in Jurassic marine rocks we find coiled fossil cephalopods called ammonites. In life, these would have looked like an octopus peeping out of a coiled shell. They evolved quickly, and we can date the different beds of Jurassic rocks from the different ammonites that they contain.

The reptiles had become so important in the Jurassic that they had developed into many different types, including flying and swimming types. The Jurassic shales and limestones contain fossil skulls, teeth, and bones of the great sea reptiles of the time. Many of these ate ammonites and fish. Fossils of the flying reptiles are found as well, because they fell into the sea when they died. Strangely enough, most of the information about land life comes from the sea-deposited rocks. An animal that dies on land usually rots away without leaving a fossil. Only if the body is washed out to sea does it become covered in sediment and have a chance to become fossilized.

**Below:** The early Jurassic rock sequence, which was called the Lias, consists of thin limestones and shales, and it is well exposed in the cliffs at Lyme Regis on the coast of Dorset, in England. This place has always been famous for its ammonite fossils, as well as for reptile fossils, such as those of the ichthyosaurs, the plesiosaurs, and the pterosaurs.

**Left:** Skeletons of the ichthyosaur fish-lizards, like those of *Stenopterygius,* lie in early Jurassic marine rocks. Sometimes the outline of the fins are seen as well.

**Right:** The first dinosaur fossil, to be recognized as that, was the *Megalosaurus* jawbone. Victorian scientists thought that it was a kind of giant lizard.

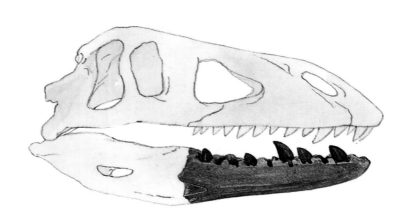

**Below:** Skeletons of early pterosaurs, such as big-headed *Dimorphodon* with its 4-foot-wide wingspan, are found in the early Jurassic rocks of southern England.

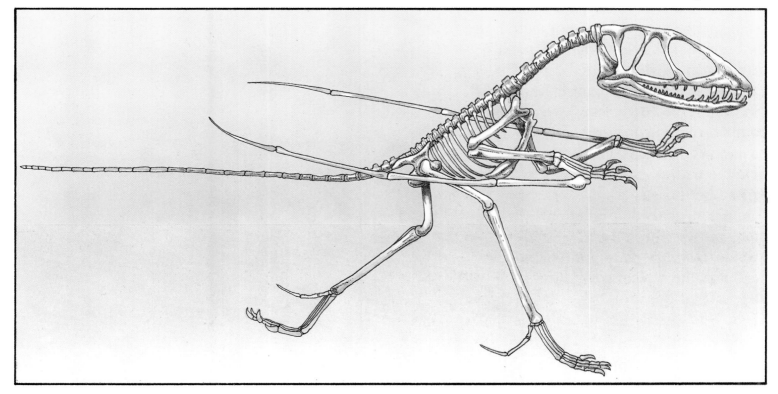

# A TIME OF SEA DRAGONS

The first studies of the early Jurassic period were done in southern England. We now know a lot about conditions in that area at the time.

The land here was low, probably consisting of scattered islands. The desert environment had given way to a much lusher landscape, as the spreading shallow seas produced moist climates. Scraps of fossil plants show that the vegetation consisted mostly of conifers and ferns. Along the beaches there would have been ammonites washed up, just as we would find seashells today. Dead sea reptiles would be washed up too, including the dolphin-like *Ichthyosaurus*. This creature had totally abandoned land life, developed a fish's tail, paddles instead of legs, and a fin on its back. It even bore its young alive, as whales do. Another sea reptile was *Plesiosaurus*. This had a squat body with paddle limbs, and a long neck with a small head. Like modern turtles it probably dragged itself ashore to lay eggs.

On land, the dinosaurs had become quite spectacular. Odd bits of teeth in the marine rocks show that big meat-eaters such as *Megalosaurus* prowled the forests. Armored plant-eating dinosaurs lived here, too. Two almost complete *Scelidosaurus* skeletons have been found. Probably the armor held the bodies intact when they drifted out to sea.

In the air the flying reptiles – the pterosaurs – wheeled and chased insects. *Dimorphodon* with its big head was the typical early Jurassic pterosaur of this area.

# EARLY JURASSIC

**Left:** The early Jurassic seas of southern England were infested with ammonites and fish, that were eaten by plesiosaurs such as *Cryptocleidus,* and the fish-lizard, *Ichthyosaurus.* Dinosaurs, such as *Megalosaurus,* prowled on the shores nearby, while pterosaurs, like *Dimorphodon,* wheeled in the sky and hunted for insects.

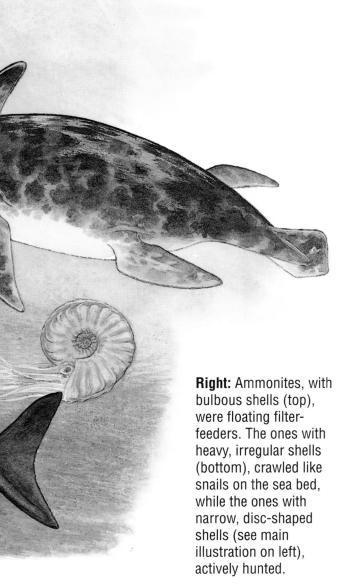

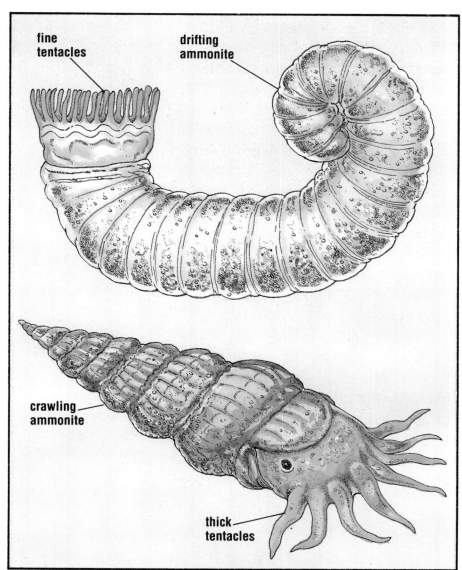

fine tentacles

drifting ammonite

crawling ammonite

thick tentacles

**Right:** Ammonites, with bulbous shells (top), were floating filter-feeders. The ones with heavy, irregular shells (bottom), crawled like snails on the sea bed, while the ones with narrow, disc-shaped shells (see main illustration on left), actively hunted.

# LATE JURASSIC STORYBOOK

The most famous dinosaurs lived in North America in the late Jurassic period. At that time, a shallow sea spread southward through the center of the continent. To the west, the Rocky Mountains were already in existence. Streams and rivers flowed off these mountains eastward to the sea. They laid down river sands and gravels, building up a broad, well-watered plain. Today, these sands and gravels are found, turned to stone, in a long belt stretching from New Mexico to Wyoming. In Colorado, they form a distinctive ridge along the foot of the modern Rockies. It was in these rocks that the most spectacular dinosaur discoveries were made in the latter half of last century.

These are river-deposited rocks, and show the usual S-shaped curve in the bed. There are also layers of the mineral calcite in the form that we find today in well-drained tropical soils in India and Australia. This all suggests a dry warm plain with rivers meandering across, and occasionally flooding. Skeletons preserved here are of animals that lived along the banks of the rivers. The most complete skeletons are of those that fell into the rivers and were quickly buried. Those that died on land were chewed up and scattered by scavenging animals before floods buried them in sand and silt.

The same conditions in East Africa produced the same kinds of rocks. We find the same kinds of animals preserved in them. This shows that Pangea was still whole at that time, and the same kinds of animals lived over the whole world.

**Above:** The best dinosaur fossils in North America are found in the famous Morrison Formation along the eastern edge of the Rocky Mountains. Bones and, often, whole skeletons are preserved in river sandstones. At Dinosaur National Monument in Utah, visitors can see the excavation of dinosaur bones. The Morrison Formation has yielded dinosaur bones for the last one hundred years.

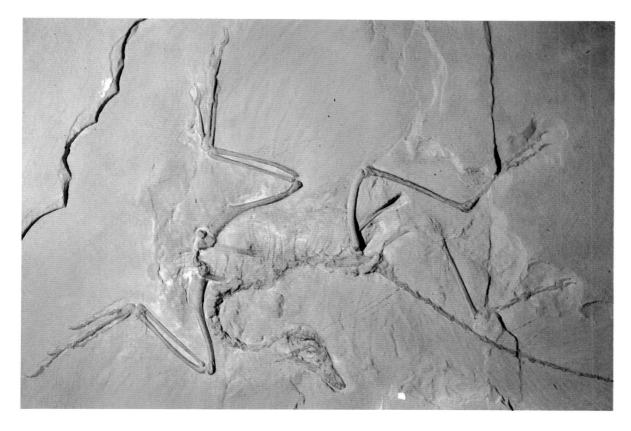

**Left:** A sequence of very fine limestones at Solnhofen in Germany gives very detailed, late Jurassic fossils. Its most famous fossil is that of *Archaeopteryx*, the first bird. It even shows the feathers that clothed the little, dinosaur-like body.

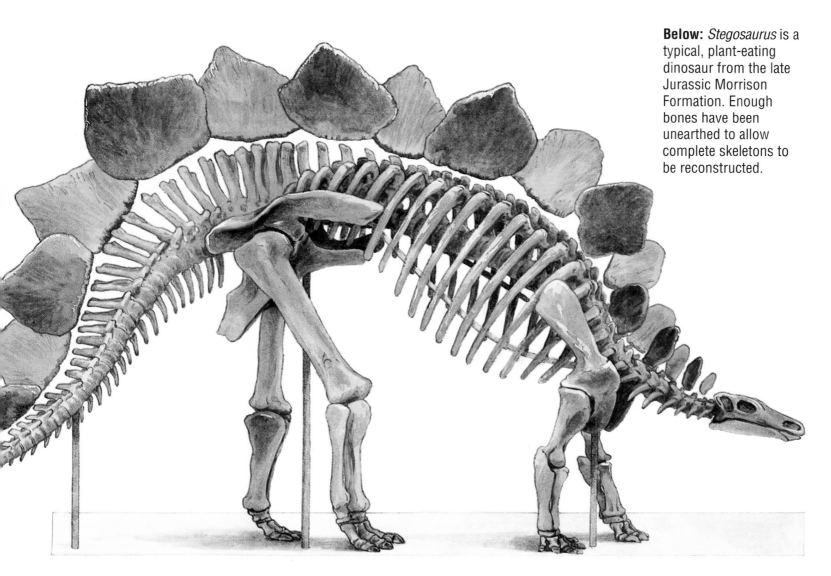

**Below:** *Stegosaurus* is a typical, plant-eating dinosaur from the late Jurassic Morrison Formation. Enough bones have been unearthed to allow complete skeletons to be reconstructed.

# THE HEYDAY OF THE DINOSAURS

Between the jagged range of the young Rocky Mountains and the warm inland sea – called the Sundance Sea – lies a well-watered plain, criss-crossed by winding rivers and streams. The region supports a sward of low ferny plants, with isolated clumps and riverside stands of conifers and tree ferns.

Browsing among these trees are herds of enormous dinosaurs. They all have the same general shape – bodies and legs like elephants, long swaying necks, tiny heads, and whip-like tails. There are many different kinds – long narrow types such as *Diplodocus* and *Apatosaurus* that can rear up on their hind legs to reach the high branches, and more solid types with necks that tower up from their high shoulders, such as *Brachiosaurus* and

**Above:** Birds evolved in the late Jurassic. *Archaeopteryx* had a bird's feathers and wings, but a reptile's head, hands, and tail.

*Camarasaurus.* When these herds move from one clump of trees to another, they guard their vulnerable young in the center. We know this by the footprints that they have left.

The footprints also tell us that they were stalked by meat-eaters. Fierce hunters such as 20-foot long *Ceratosaurus* hunted in packs. When they killed an unwary plant-eater, they ate their fill and moved on. Bigger meat-eaters such as 36-foot long *Allosaurus* then came and ate most of what was left. The remaining scraps were eaten up by smaller dinosaurs such as *Coelurus*, less than 6 feet long, and the many pterosaurs. Chewed-up bones of plant-eating dinosaurs mixed with teeth from different meat-eaters are found throughout the Jurassic deposits.

**Left:** The very long, plant-eating dinosaurs, such as 88 foot *Diplodocus,* could rear up and browse on vegetation 49 feet above the ground. Its light build, its snaky neck, and its heavy concentration of muscles over its hips helped it to do this.

**Left:** Herds of plant-eating dinosaurs, like *Brachiosaurus,* wandered along the wooded river banks of late Jurassic North America. They were in constant danger from fierce meat-eating types, such as the horned *Ceratosaurus.*

**Left:** Heavier, squatter plant-eaters, such as 59 foot *Camarasaurus,* had necks that reached up into the trees from their high shoulders.

# EARLY CRETACEOUS STORYBOOK

The dinosaur age reached its climax in the Cretaceous period, 144 to 65 million years ago. As with the other periods, we know most about the Cretaceous from detailed studies of well-exposed rocks in a particular area. Southern England, Belgium, and northern France are the best areas for early Cretaceous land fossils.

Here, sandstones and clays that were laid down in a huge fresh-water lake that covered the area are found. The kinds of sand grains tell us where the sand was washed from and what the surrounding landscape was like. Scraps of plant fossils show what kind of vegetation grew inland. The sandstone is quarried for building blocks and road stone, and in these quarries, in the 1820s, the first dinosaur bones to be studied properly were found. The bones were of the famous plant-eater *Iguanodon*. About 50 years later, the skeletons of some 30 *Iguanodon* were found in a coal mine in Belgium. The coal-bearing Pennsylvanian rocks had hollows filled with Cretaceous deposits, and the skeletons had gathered in these hollows.

More recently, in 1983, a clay pit in southern England yielded a new type of early Cretaceous dinosaur. Called *Baryonyx* it had a crocodile's head and a huge claw. Fish scales were found in its stomach.

In the lake deposits there are also remains of smaller dinosaurs, crocodiles, fish, turtles, and pterosaurs. Footprints and the imprints of leathery hide show how *Iguanodon* herds wandered around and wallowed in the mud.

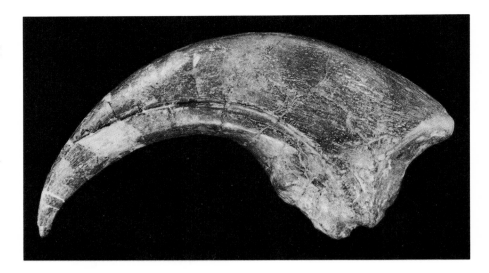

**Above:** The 1 foot claw of *Baryonyx* , that was found in the early Cretaceous clays of Surrey, in England, in 1983, showed that the skeleton of a completely new type of dinosaur lay buried there. This was the first new dinosaur that had been found in Britain for very many years.

**Above:** The three-toed footprints of *Iguanodon,* that were common in early Cretaceous lake deposits, show where very many dinosaurs had walked across the squishy mud. We also find skin marks, showing where they lay down and rolled around.

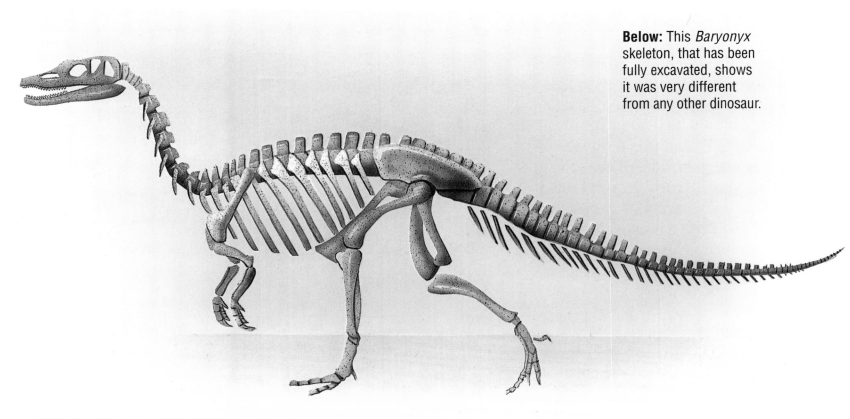

**Below:** This *Baryonyx* skeleton, that has been fully excavated, shows it was very different from any other dinosaur.

**Left:** Sea cliffs in southern England, that eroded into early Cretaceous Wealden sandstones, were favourite haunts for Victorian fossil collectors, who were searching for some evidence of dinosaurs.

# DINOSAURS AND THEIR LANDSCAPE

A huge placid lake stretches over what is now southern England and northern Europe. Along the mud banks at its edge are deep reed beds of horsetails, like those of today. On drier ground, there are forests of conifer trees and tree ferns, and clumps of palm-like plants related to the modern cycads. Beyond the forests, to the north of the lake, are ridges of Pennsylvanian limestones and coal deposits. Still further on is an upland area of even older rocks, Ordovician or Silurian, in the misty distance.

A small herd of *Iguanodon* wade knee-deep in the reed beds, heads down and grazing on the horsetails as they go. As they cross the damp mud banks in between, they leave their characteristic three-toed footprints. Ahead of them scamper several *Hypsilophodon*, looking like *Iguanodon* but only about 6 feet long and very lightly built.

In the distance, where a stream empties out into the lake, a *Baryonyx* stands, waiting patiently to hook fish out of the water with its huge claw, as modern bears do. But there are no fish today. Away upstream, in a gorge in the Pennsylvanian rocks of the hills, a herd of *Iguanodon* has been trapped by floodwaters and drowned. Their carcasses are decaying and the water is poisoned.

This is a local picture, however. Pangea has begun to break up now, and there are different landscapes on different continents in different parts of the world. North Africa, for example, has deserts, with desert-dwelling dinosaurs like the sail-backed *Spinosaurus*, a relative of *Baryonyx*.

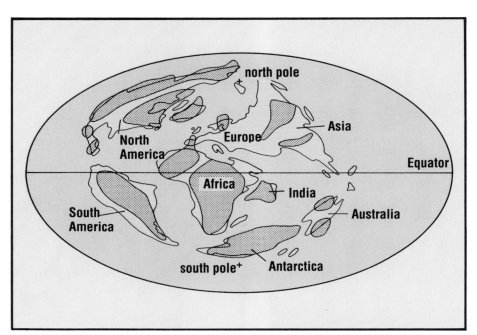

**Above:** The huge super continent had begun to break up into our modern continents by Cretaceous times.

# EARLY CRETACEOUS

**Left:** Herds of massive *Iguanodon* and sprightly, little *Hypsilophodon* browsed on the shores of the lake that covered southern England and northern Europe in the early Cretaceous period, while the fish-eating dinosaur, *Baryonyx,* dipped for its prey in the rivers and streams.

# LATE CRETACEOUS STORYBOOK

In the late Cretaceous period, Pangea was completely shattered, and most of the continents were drifting apart with new oceans opening up between. In addition, the continents themselves were again flooded by shallow seas. A very pure limestone, called chalk, was deposited in these shallow seas. Late Cretaceous chalk is found in many parts of the world, including Kansas and southern England, where it forms the famous White Cliffs of Dover.

Because the continents were now separate, the land animals had begun to evolve in different ways. The dinosaurs we find in North America are quite different from those we find in South America, and different from those in Australia, and so on.

The mud stones of Montana show that, as in the late Jurassic, there was a river plain between the Rockies and a sea that stretched north-south across the North American continent. Plant fossils show that the vegetation was then completely different. The most dramatic remains found here are those of dinosaur nests, containing eggs and young ones. There are also very good dinosaur fossils, including some with the skin preserved.

Then, in many parts of the world, there was a strange clay bed at the very top of the Cretaceous rocks. It is rich in elements that are rare on the Earth. Many scientists believe that this is evidence of a great catastrophe – that a giant meteorite or a swarm of comets struck the Earth and caused so much damage that all the dinosaurs died out.

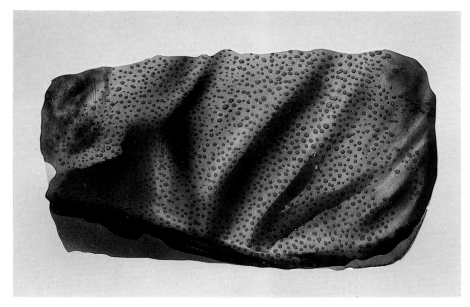

**Above**: A group of dinosaurs, called the duckbills, were common in late Cretaceous North America. Impressions of their skin show that they had a rough, scaly appearance.

**Left:** Duckbill nests, like this model, have been found in late Cretaceous rocks. Many nests would be built in the same area. Each consisted of a mound of mud about 5 foot high, with a shallow depression in the top. The eggs were laid in a bed of vegetation. Skeletons of very young dinosaurs were also found in the nests, and this gave some clues to the family life of the duck-billed dinosaurs.

**Below:** Duck-billed fossils have even been found with their skin on! The imprint of skin was preserved when the body was buried quickly in a river bed. This fossil, *Anatosaurus,* is lying on its side, the head towards us and one forelimb in the air. The skin, that was stretched over the ribs, can be seen clearly in this illustration.

# THE CLIMAX OF THE DINOSAURS

The last of the dinosaurs were the strangest. Some had horns on their heads and shields on their necks, such as *Triceratops*, while others were armored all over, such as *Ankylosaurus*.

The most successful were probably the duck-billed dinosaurs. These were related to *Iguanodon* and spread over western North America and Asia at the end of the Cretaceous. From their well-preserved fossils we can see that they could walk on their hind legs or on all fours, and had long deep tails. Some had crests on their heads that were used for signaling. They lived near water, and it used to be thought that they were swimming animals. The nests that have been found belong to duckbills called *Maiasaura*. They were heaps of mud, like crocodile nests, and whole herds of *Maiasaura* nested together. The youngsters stayed in the nest, being looked after, until they were quite well grown. They nested on forested river banks. The plants had now changed. Instead of ferns and cycads, there were modern flowers and trees, such as willow, oak, and magnolia.

Elsewhere, in the shallow seas that covered central North America and northern Europe, the sea reptiles reached their climax as well. The ichthyosaurs had gone now, and were replaced by giant sea lizards such as *Tylosaurus*. Plesiosaurs were still around, such as long-necked *Elasmosaurus* and the whale-like *Kronosaurus*. Many of these fed on ammonites that were still common, and the fish that, like the plants, had evolved into modern types.

**Below**: From the evidence of fossil skeletons – skin and nests that were unearthed in the Two Medicine Formation of Montana – we can see how a duckbill at its nesting site appeared. The herd had nested on the banks of a river, as it wound its way through trees and bushes.

# LATE CRETACEOUS

**Above:** Other late Cretaceous dinosaurs included heavily armored forms, such as *Euoplocephalus,* that had a club on its tail and spikes on its back for its defense.

**Below:** The horned dinosaurs were among the last. *Triceratops* had three horns on its head, and a huge, armored frill on its neck.

**Above:** The biggest meat-eating dinosaurs lived at this time. The most famous was 39-foot *Tyrannosaurus.*

# TERTIARY STORYBOOK

Above the level of the bed of clay that is thought to mark the impact of the giant meteorite that may have hit the Earth at the end of the Cretaceous period, the rocks are quite different and contain totally different fossils. There are not any dinosaurs in these rocks, no great sea reptiles, no pterosaurs, no ammonites. All of these had become extinct by the end of the Cretaceous. The younger rocks belong to a period called the Tertiary, from 65 to 1.7 million years ago.

Many of the Tertiary rocks are so young that they have not had time to be turned into stone. The soft clays of eastern England are very much as they were when they were laid down in a shallow sea about 50 million years ago. They contain fossils such as sharks' teeth and seashells that have altered very little in that time. In other places, the Tertiary rocks are quite solid. In Germany and Poland, for example, there are deposits of brown coal, representing the remains of old cypress swamps. This brown coal is softer and peatier than the black coals of the Pennsylvanian period because it has not been buried so deep or for so long.

Most of the continents were more or less in their present positions during the Tertiary. India and Australia, however, were drifting northward quite quickly. Africa ground up against Europe, throwing up the Alps and producing the twisted shape of the Mediterranean Sea. India finally collided with Asia to produce what is currently the greatest range of mountains on Earth – The Himalayas.

**Above:** The late Tertiary period saw the rise of grassland animals, including many rhinoceros-like forms. Great numbers of skeletons of *Brontotherium* – 10 feet long and 8 feet high – have been found in the plains of North America, where they once roamed in vast herds.

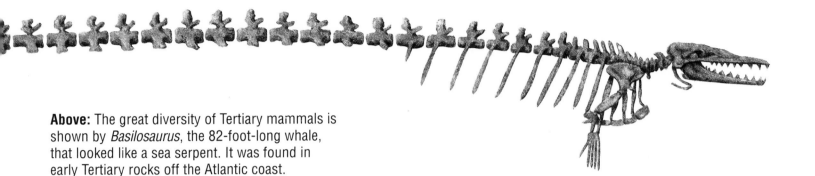

**Above:** The great diversity of Tertiary mammals is shown by *Basilosaurus*, the 82-foot-long whale, that looked like a sea serpent. It was found in early Tertiary rocks off the Atlantic coast.

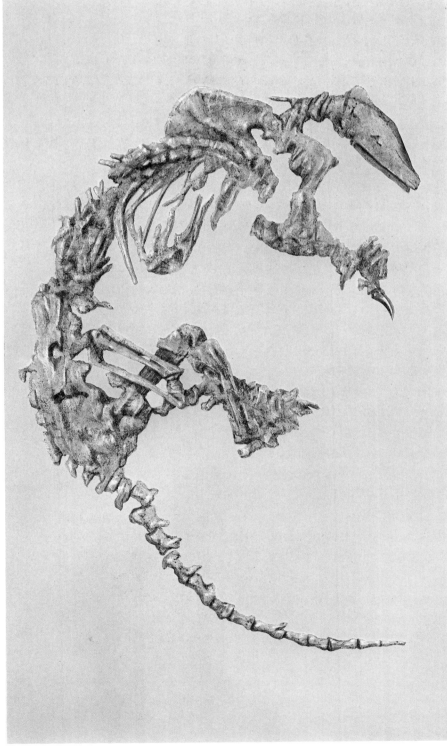

**Right:** Some of the forest animals that evolved in the early Tertiary period, were so successful that they have survived almost unchanged until today. The German anteater, *Eurotamandua,* is almost identical to the collared anteater, that is found in the South America of today.

# THE MAMMALS TAKE OVER

The dinosaurs died out at the end of the Cretaceous period. We do not really know why. Possibly a meteorite struck the Earth and caused such a change to the climate and vegetation that none of the big animals could survive. On the other hand, it may have been the movement of continents that caused these changes in climate and vegetation. Whatever happened, the big reptiles had vanished.

The mammals then took over. Ever since they evolved in the Triassic period, the mammals were small shrew-like creatures that scuttled around the dinosaurs' feet, never amounting to much. Now, with the reptiles gone, they expanded and took up the reptiles' life styles. Rhinoceros-like mammals took over from the big plant-eating dinosaurs. Fierce wolf-like mammals took over from the meat-eaters. Bats took over from the pterosaurs. Whales took over from the plesiosaurs, and so on.

In some places, such as the north-European coal fields, we find a very well-preserved selection of mammals. We even find ants preserved that are very similar to modern ants. Feeding on them were anteaters, such as *Eurotamandua* and *Eomanis*, that were very much like the modern anteaters and pangolins.

The climate was quite warm and moist throughout most of the world, and thick forests grew in most places. All kinds of new mammals developed on the various continents, but in the early Tertiary they were mostly forest-dwelling animals. This was soon to change.

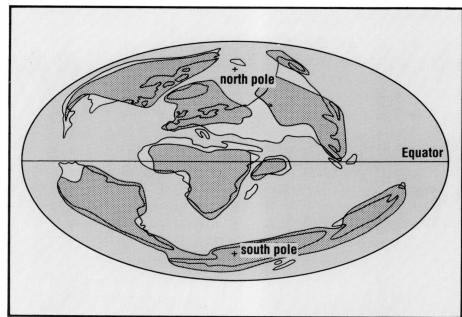

**Above:** The continents were more or less in their present positions, by the Tertiary period.

**Left:** *Basilosaurus,* the sea-serpent-like whale, dove for squid in the Atlantic Ocean, as do modern sperm whales.

**Left:** Southern Germany, 50 million years ago, had swamps similar to the modern subtropical cypress swamps of North America. Many insect-eating animals, such as the anteater, *Eurotamandua,* and the early pangolin, *Eomanis,* scratched in the plant debris for their food. Even the ants have been found preserved.

# RUNNING MAMMALS EVOLVE

About halfway through the Tertiary period the landscape began to change again. Grasses evolved. The forests dwindled, and in their place the world's great grasslands spread. Prairie, savanna, steppe, and pampas opened up over the continents.

The mammal life evolved to keep pace. Forest browsers became open landscape grazers. Grass is a very tough food. It needs especially hard-wearing or easily replaced teeth and a heavy-duty digestive system to cope with it. Living on open plains, an animal can see danger coming from far off, and this encourages the evolution of long-legged running animals. The hoofed animals that are so familiar today – the horses, antelope, camels, and pigs – began to develop. From their remains, we can trace the evolution of the horse from a small rabbit-like forest browser to the familiar plains grazer. Camels evolved very quickly into all sorts of grassland forms, including tall giraffe-like types and lightweight antelope-like forms. Today, we only have specialized desert-living and mountain-living camels, and the zebras are the only successful wild horses left. The places of these animals have been taken by the more recently-evolved antelopes, goats, and cows.

While all this was happening among the mammals, a similar evolution was taking place among the birds. They took up the wide range of life styles that they have today, some even adopting a flightless, plains-living existence like that of the modern ostrich.

**Above:** Huge, running birds, such as *Phorusrhacus,* evolved to hunt on the Tertiary grasslands of South America.

**Right:** The rhinoceros. shape was a shape that evolved early. The giant *Brontotherium* grazed on the grassy plains of North America.

**Left:** The plains of late Tertiary North America supported herds of horses, like *Pliohippus*, and camels, like the tall *Aepycamelus*. Various kinds of elephants lived here too, like the shovel-tusked *Amebelodon*, which scooped up pond weed from the water holes.
*Epigaulus*, a burrowing rodent, was also present, and was the only one with horns. It had broad front feet and powerful claws.

# QUATERNARY STORYBOOK

The last 1.7 million years of the Earth's history is called the Quaternary period. The big event of the time was the great Ice Age, and this finished a mere 10,000 years ago.

Several times the ice swept outward from the poles and down from the mountains, covering large areas of Europe, northern Asia, and North America with ice sheets thousands of yards thick. The evidence is everywhere in these regions. As the ice sheets and glaciers inched forward, they tore rocks away from their beds and hollowed out the landscape. When the ice retreated, the rocky debris was left as hills and ridges of rubble and clay, and the hollows filled with water and became lakes. Valleys were gouged out into deep U-shapes. The weight of the ice pressed the land downward so that the sea formed new beaches that now lie well above sea level.

Then, time after time, the ice retreated and the climate became warmer than it is now. The bones of hippopotamuses and elephants are found in deposits by the River Thames in London, England. Later, after a few tens of thousands of years, the ice crept back again to give yet another phase of cold climate in the Ice Age.

The varying water temperatures encouraged the growth of different microscopic sea animals at various times. By looking at their remains in the successive layers of mud on the sea bed, we can tell that the ice came and went about twenty times during the Quaternary period.

**Right:** The frozen mud of the Ice Age has often refrigerated and preserved the bodies of drowned mammoths, such as this 12,000-year-old baby, that was found in the Soviet Union.

**Above:** Moving ice wears down the rocks over which it travels. The smooth surface of this rock outcrop in Greenland was polished by action of glaciers.

**Above:** Much of the modern landscape was carved by the ice of the Ice Age. The great weight of valley glaciers ground out their valleys into deep U-shapes, as here in Switzerland.

**Right:** The skeletons of some Ice Age mammals, such as this giant ground sloth, look so fresh that they could have lived at the same time as early man.

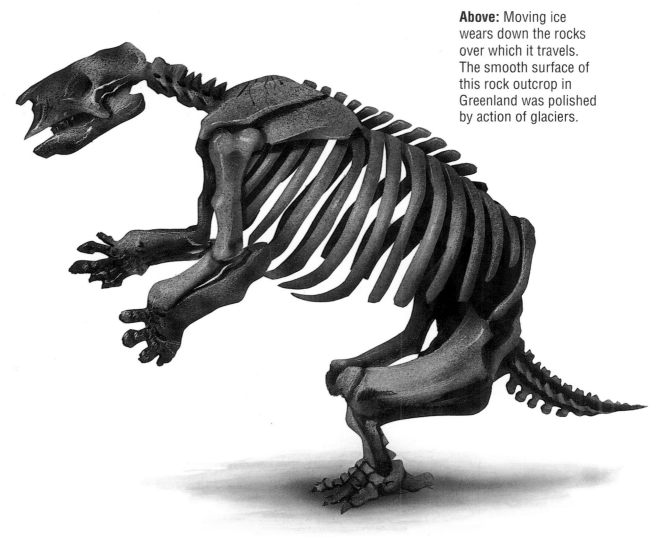

# THE ICE AGE

**D**uring the coldest times of the Quaternary period, the north polar ice cap was much larger than it is now. It spread on to the northern continents. Outward from the edge of this were vast areas of tundra – the boggy treeless wasteland with the permanently frozen subsoil that we now find in the far north of Siberia, Alaska, and Canada. Across this bleak landscape there strode the woolly elephants called mammoths, and the long-horned woolly rhinoceros. Their great size and shaggy coats helped them to resist the cold. The great Irish elk, with antlers that spread 10 feet, also lived here, grazing on the tough grasses and lichens.

When the glaciers retreated and warmer climates prevailed, a more recognizable fauna developed. The

**Above:** Glaciers covered much of the northern hemisphere, during the Quaternary Ice Age.

kinds of animals that we now get in the tropical forests and grasslands of Africa then lived in Europe.

Meanwhile, in South America, there were different animals altogether. South America had been an island for most of the Tertiary and strange animals had evolved there. Giant ground sloths 13 feet high fed from treetops. Huge armadillo-like beasts as big as our cars grazed the grasslands. Then the land bridge of Central America was squeezed up and the two American continents were joined. The North American animals flooded southward and began to compete with the native creatures. All these strange South American animals were wiped out and replaced by the more successful North American types.

**Above:** *Glyptodon* was one of the 6 foot and 5 inch long, armadillo-like beasts from South America.

**Below:** The gigantic *Megatherium* was the biggest of the giant ground sloths.

**Left:** Cold-weather beasts of the tundra, protected by their large size and shaggy coats, included *Megaloceros,* the great Irish elk, *Coelodonta,* the woolly rhinoceros, and the mammoth, *Mammuthus.*

# THE EARLIEST MEN

One of the groups of mammals that came into being at the beginning of the Tertiary period was the primate group. These include the lemurs, the monkeys, and, later, the apes.

They were always a specialized tree-living group, feeding on leaves and fruit, and also on insects. When the grasslands developed halfway through the Tertiary, they remained tree-dwellers and kept to the forest areas. The line that gave rise to the modern apes and, ultimately, to ourselves can be traced back to *Dryopithecus*. This was a very ape-like creature that lived in the trees of Europe, Asia, and Africa in the middle Tertiary. As the climate of eastern Africa became drier at the end of the Tertiary, the forests that remained dwindled. The apes of the area were forced to spend much of their time on the ground, moving from one clump of trees to another. While on the ground, they walked upright, both to enable them to see over the long grass and to allow winds to cool them under the fierce glare of the sun.

Soon a ground-dwelling ape called *Australopithecus* evolved. There were several species of *Australopithecus*. Some were gorilla-like, with heavy jaws, and ate seeds and nuts. Another was much more lightly built and could eat both plants and animals, which they hunted in packs, by acting as teams.

The next stage came when these hunting apes developed the ability to make simple tools. This was when they progressed from ape to man – *Homo habilis*, handy man.

**Left:** *Australopithecus,* the "southern ape" of eastern and southern Africa, hunted in groups for animals, that were stronger and faster than itself. It could pick up stones and sticks and use them as tools and weapons. There were several species of *Australopithecus,* but the one that hunted animals was the most successful.

**Above:** The first true humans evolved from the successful *Australopithecus. Homo habilis*, or "handy man", was able to make his own tools.

**Right:** *Homo erectus* was the first widely-ranging human, and these tribes migrated from Africa into Europe and Asia. They discovered the secret of fire and used it for cooking and keeping warm.

# HUMANS ARRIVE

From *Homo habilis* in East Africa there developed the first widespread human. We call him *Homo erectus* – upright man – and his remains are found in Africa and across Eurasia from Spain to Java. He must have looked very much like a modern human in build and posture, but he still had ape-like brow ridges and protruding jaws. The brain, however, was almost as big as that of a modern human. He was an accomplished tool-maker, and he had discovered the secret of making and using fire. He built tent-like huts from brushwood supported on a framework of poles. He lived from 1.6 million to about 200,000 years ago.

His successor was *Homo sapiens* – thinking man. There were two sub-species that we call Cro-Magnon man, after the place in France where his remains were found, and Neanderthal man, after the Neander Valley in Germany where his remains first came to light. Neanderthal man was somewhat heavier in appearance than Cro-Magnon man and still had heavy eyebrows and jaws.

It was Cro-Magnon man who survived to become modern man. Not only was he very clever in a scientific way, in his tool-making, and so on, but he was an artist as well. Caves both in central France and in northern Spain are famous for the beautiful paintings that he did of the animals he saw around him.

Today, we think of ourselves as the pinnacle of life. Yet we have only recently arrived after 3,500 million years of evolution. The life of our planet will continue to evolve long after we have gone.

**Below:** Human beings were able to make use of the resources they found, wherever they spread. *Homo sapiens*, or "thinking man", hunted mammoths, woolly rhinoceros, and reindeer during the latter part of the Ice Age. They ate their meat, used their skins for clothing and shelter, and made tools, buildings, and ornaments out of their bones. In this way, they were able to colonize the bleakest corners of this bitterly cold tundra landscape.

**Above:** *Homo sapiens neanderthalensis*, one of the subspecies of the Ice Age humans, did not survive. They probably disappeared by interbreeding with the more successful subspecies of that time.

**Above:** *Homo sapiens sapiens* was the more successful subspecies. This subspecies survives to this day, and is the one to which we, ourselves, belong.

Figures in **bold** refer to captions.

# ACKNOWLEDGMENTS

**ILLUSTRATIONS**

**Peter Bull Art Studio** 7 top, 17 right, 20 top, 21 top, 23 right, 26 bottom, 27 bottom, 29 bottom, 36 bottom, 40 bottom, 49 bottom, 51 bottom right;
**Ian Fleming Associates/John Butler** 20–21 bottom, 24–25, 46–47, 47 top, 54, 55 center, 55 bottom, 58–59;
**Brian McIntyre** 4–5, 6–7, 28, 29 top, 30–31, 34–35, 35 right, 38 bottom left, 38–39, 42–43, 43 top, 63 top, 63 center, 63 bottom, 64–65 top, 64–65 bottom, 65 right, 66–67, 67 right; **John Rogers** 32 bottom, 33 top, 57 top, 60 top, 60–61, 61 top, 68 top, 68–69, 69 top, 71 bottom, 72–73, 73 top, 73 bottom, 74–75, 75 top, 75 bottom, 76–77, 77 top, 77 bottom;
**Hamlyn Publishing** 10 top, 11, 24 top, 30 top, 38 top, 42 top, 46 top, 58 top, 66 top, 72 top; **David Johnston** 70 bottom; **Martin Knowelden** 62–63; **Janos Marffy** 9;
**Ann Winterbotham** 12–13, 14, 16–17, 41 top, 41 bottom, 48, 49 center, 50–51, 53 bottom.

**PHOTOGRAPHIC**

The publishers would like to thank the following organizations and individuals for their kind permission to reproduce the photographs in this book.
British Museum (Natural History), London 56 top;
Bruce Coleman Limited/Patrick Baker 13 bottom;
Mary Evans Picture Library/F Briggs 57 bottom;
G.S.F. Picture Library 10 bottom, 19 top left, 37 bottom left, 49 top, 52, 56 bottom, 70–71 top, 71 top right;
Robert Harding Picture Library/A C Waltham 45 top;
S. Conway Morris 15 top;
Nature Photographers Ltd/Nicholas Brown 8 center; S C Bisserot 8 top;
RIDA Photo Library/David Bayliss 18 bottom, 19 top right, 19 bottom, 22–23, 33 bottom left, 33 right, 36 top, 37 top, 37 bottom right, 40–41 top; R C L Wilson 37 center left;
Science Photo Library/Michael Marten 26–27 top; Sinclair Stammers 18 top, 32 top, 53 top;
H B Whittington 15 bottom;
ZEFA/H Helmlinger 8 bottom; Colin Maher 45 bottom; Dr F Sauer 44.